Presented To:

_____

From:

_____

Date:

_____

DESTINY IMAGE BOOKS BY KEVIN DEDMON

The Ultimate Treasure Hunt

Unlocking Heaven

THE
RISK
FACTOR

**CROSSING THE CHICKEN LINE INTO
YOUR SUPERNATURAL DESTINY**

KEVIN DEDMON &
CHAD DEDMON

DESTINY IMAGE® PUBLISHERS, INC.

P.O. Box 310, Shippensburg, PA 17257-0310

"Promoting Inspired Live."

This book and all other Destiny Image, Revival Press, MercyPlace, Fresh Bread, Destiny Image Fiction, and Treasure House books are available at Christian bookstores and distributors worldwide.

For a U.S. bookstore nearest you, call 1-800-722-6774.

For more information on foreign distributors, call 717-532-3040.

Reach us on the Internet: www.destinyimage.com.

ISBN 13 TP: 978-0-7684-4092-8
ISBN 13 Ebook: 978-0-7684-8875-3

For Worldwide Distribution, Printed in the U.S.A.

1 2 3 4 5 6 7 8 / 15 14 13 12 11

ACKNOWLEDGMENTS

We would like to thank our family—mother Theresa, Alexa, and Julia for partnering with us on this wild adventure of risk, encouraging us to take extreme levels of risk along the way. Each one in our family have continually stepped into our supernatural destiny through amazing feats of risk, which has pushed the risk envelope in new ways that we could have never achieved, or even would have attempted, on our own.

Thanks to Bill and Beni Johnson and Kris and Kathy Vallotton, who has paved the way for dreaming big, and empowering us to go for it. Your example has encouraged us to believe that we can do the impossible.

Thanks to Heidi and Rolland Baker, who are the forerunners of risk to our generation. You have taught us that there is "always enough" when we take risk to release the Kingdom of God.

Thanks to Pam Spinosi, our "grammar doctor," who keeps us word healthy, happy, and whole.

Once again, thanks to Julia for helping Chad during the long nights of writing and editing. It truly was a labor of love that I will never forget. You are amazing!

Finally, thanks to all the ministry partners we have worked with over the years, and churches who have given us the freedom to step out into our supernatural destiny.

ENDORSEMENTS

Kevin and Chad Dedmon have co-written an exciting book that contains the steps needed to living a life in the supernatural. This is not theory, this book has been tested in the real world and found workable. This book will teach you how to come up to the chicken line, take the risk to release your faith, and step into the supernatural power of God. A very encouraging book for those no longer satisfied with the mundane, who want to become co-laborers with the God of the Universe. A great read.

RANDY CLARK

Fear has caused so many of us to settle for a mundane, boring and meaningless existence. Our need for the great adventure is being siphoned off by virtual reality as we escape deep into the fantasy world of video games, Internet and television. It's here that we have exchanged the authentic desire to be a hero and to live on the edge;

for predictable scripts, plastic plants and computer-generated stunts. Think about it folks, what great message will be inscribed on our tombstones, "Here lies a man who watched movies." The truth is that our inner man hungers to really live, to take a risk and to be a part of something worth dying for.

In their book, *The Risk Factor,* Kevin and Chad Dedmon challenge us to "step over the chicken line," and take hold of our divine destiny. I have known both of these men for more than ten years. This father and son team is like the dynamic duo; real life superheroes who have spent the last several years living at extreme risk. Their testimonies are almost unbelievable and their lives are full of zeal. Whether you are a bored, visionless Believer or a passionate Christian who needs to learn the skill of stepping out in faith…this book is for you! BUT BEWARE!!! This book could get you off the couch and put your life at risk!

Kris Vallotton
Co-Founder of Bethel School of Supernatural Ministry
Author of seven books including, *The Supernatural Ways of Royalty*
Senior Associate Leader of Bethel Church, Redding, California

In my life and ministry I have rarely met such amazing risk takers as Kevin and Chad Dedmon. They are perfectly suited to write this book because their lives give us courage by the very choices they make all the time. They both have a unique perspective in their faith to live life with a full "yes" to God and they are catalytic in their inspirational journey: thus the book is born out of real examples. If you want to truly be radical this book will impart a zeal and skill set to change the very foundation of how you live.

Shawn Bolz
Senior Pastor of Expression58
Author of *Keys to Heaven's Economy* &
The Nonreligious Guide to Dating

Marrying a determined faith missionary with no fear like Heidi was a big risk. Going off to the mission field with no support or return ticket was a big risk. Facing machine guns, hijackers, killers and witch doctors every day in Mozambique was a big risk. Taking in hundreds of children with no food to feed them was a big risk. Telling naive bush villages that Jesus would heal their blind and deaf was a big risk. But we got revival. Kevin and Chad have figured out something, and Heidi and I identify with them! If you want to play it safe, read another book. If you want crazy, fiery encouragement, read this one!!

ROLLAND BAKER
Director, Iris Ministries
Mozambique, Africa

Few people I know lead in the lifestyle of risk and faith than the Dedmon's. This father/son combo is the perfect one-two punch to get you to 'cross the chicken-line'. You will find few other resources that stimulate your faith the way this book does. Kevin and Chad are two of the most catalytic people I've ever known. This book is a must-read for those wanting to enter or expand their life of faith and risk. Entire leadership communities need to read and do what are in these pages!

DANNY SILK
Author of *Loving Our Kids on Purpose* and *Culture of Honor*

CONTENTS

Foreword by ▶▶ **BILL JOHNSON**

This book is very important, but for more reasons than you might think. You'll no doubt be inspired and greatly impacted by the content. Both of these men live what they teach, which gives them an unusual authority to impart the grace to do as they teach. But what amazes me most about *The Risk Factor* is the timing. This is the third father-son book that has come from our staff in the last year: the other two are *The Supernatural Power of Forgiveness*, by Jason and Kris Vallotton, and *Momentum*, by my son Eric and me. This phenomenon was not orchestrated by anyone other than the Holy Spirit. We never sat down with a plan to invade the market with father/son books. I wouldn't have thought of it. There may be many such books in church history, but I don't remember ever having seen one in my years of following the Lord. Why do I consider this to be so important? It reveals an unusual season: now is the time for the partnership of multiple generations to live and work together in honor, celebrating each other, all while invading realms that have been considered impossible by previous generations.

Kevin and Chad are the real deal. Kevin, already a successful pastor, brought his family to Redding to attend Bethel School of Supernatural Ministry (BSSM). He wasn't satisfied with what he had learned in the traditional form of ministry training. It's that kind of humility that God takes note of, when a pastor becomes a student, sometimes sitting next to someone in class who has been saved for maybe six months. This approach to life is part of the background story to the risk lifestyle illustrated throughout these pages.

Chad is also a graduate of our BSSM. His lifestyle of risk became more and more evident through his years in Redding, providing us with some of the more exciting testimonies of God's intervention for people in non-traditional settings. He has become one of our star students because of his faithfulness to live with risk, but also to live with honor. He and his wife have done so well, inspiring countless numbers of people. This whole approach to life is a dream come true for me. I had always hoped that miracles would happen in public places as they did for Jesus. But the only model I had seen was inside the church. As much as I celebrate the move of God anywhere, my heart ached for "marketplace" impact of the kingdom. I can honestly say that more miracles now happen outside of the four walls of the church than inside, and they are continuous inside. And a large part of the reason for this is a generation of Kevins and Chads, who are willing to risk all to see what God would do that the name of Jesus would be held in highest esteem by our communities.

The Risk Factor will challenge and stretch every reader until the desire for breakthrough outweighs the fear of risk. *The Risk Factor* will also instruct, inspire, and direct anyone with even a slight interest in miracles as a lifestyle.

With great pleasure I commend to you Kevin and Chad as men who have become the Risk Factors. The book is a mere reflection of two lives lived well. It is an essential book "for such a time as this."

Bill Johnson
Senior Pastor, Bethel Church
Author of *When Heaven Invades Earth* and
Face to Face with God

Foreword by >> HEIDI BAKER

People don't want just to be told about love, unless they can see and feel it. They don't want just to hear about faith, unless it changes something in their lives. Love is not an empty concept or theory. It looks like something tangible, and the world is hungry to know what that is. Radical love requires radical acts of faith to be meaningful. It is often inconvenient and interrupts our day. It pushes us to believe for the impossible, challenges our comfort zones and compels us to take risks we wouldn't normally have the courage to take.

A few years ago we were faced with a great tragedy. We had a cholera outbreak on one of our bases in Mozambique. Eighty of our people were dying in the hospital, which was actually a tent that was referred to as "the dying tent." Cholera is dangerously contagious, but as I desperately sought the Lord, He clearly showed me what I had to do. I had to go and hug the dying, face-to-face and cheek-to-cheek!

So I went to the tent and miraculously I was able to enter freely, even though it was off-limits to everyone other than medical staff. I walked straight past the guards and through the barrier without being stopped. I held each adult and child in my arms, loving them as they vomited and defecated on me. I looked into their eyes and felt their suffering and pain. I held all of our children and pastors, and then I went and held everybody else in the hospital and led them to Jesus. A doctor named Joanna yelled at me and told me that I would die, but I declared that we would all live and not die! Perfect love casts out fear, and it takes risks that often don't make any sense in the natural. Within a few days the entire tent hospital was cleared out. Everyone was healed and Doctor Joanna came to work at our medical clinic!

To see huge supernatural breakthroughs, we need supernaturally huge hearts of love. Unless we allow Jesus to place His living heart of compassion and mercy within us, we will not have the courage to take risks to step into more of the miraculous. We all need to be continually filled with this unending, undying, tenacious love that causes us to stop and see the person God places in front of us daily. We need to flow out of a place of radical passion and compassion that doesn't focus on the problem or the cost, but compels us to action, regardless of inconvenience or discomfort. We take risks because we love, and we continue to take risks every day because we continue to choose love! The Father wants to bring every child home to be with Him, and He wants to set the suffering free. This is the simple message of the Gospel that we are called to demonstrate. This is the Good News! And we have the amazing privilege and joy of partnering with Jesus as He gathers His sons and daughter into His Kingdom from every tribe, tongue and nation.

Jesus is raising up a mighty army of laid-down lovers with supernaturally huge, shoulder-to-shoulder hearts that beat in rhythm with

His. They beat to the rhythm of compassion, mercy and love. This army of abandoned worshipers no longer fear the cost or the discomfort of loving wholeheartedly. Instead they move in extravagant acts of kindness that cause the world to take notice. They fearlessly lay their hands on the sick and run into the darkness to carry His glorious light. I pray that through this book Jesus will compel many more to become passionate, fearless lovers that move in radical, bold, risk-taking love that shakes the nations!

The Risk Factor is full of awesome testimonies that will fill your heart with great courage to step into your own lifestyle of risk-taking faith. It is a must-read for anyone who has wondered how they could step into doing the works that Jesus did, and has dared to dream of stepping into "even greater works than these." Within this book you will find the practical and spiritual tools you need to be able to step beyond your current limitations and be launched into new levels of the supernatural and the miraculous.

Kevin and Chad's lifestyles of great faith are a rich inspiration to me personally, and it is a delight to have them both as friends. Chad is an awesome spiritual son who carries a contagious enthusiasm for Jesus and relentlessly presses in for the impossible to become the possible. His hunger and thirst for the supernatural is provoking a generation of believers not to settle for anything less than the fullness of their inheritance. I have seen Kevin and Chad pour their lives into others without reservation so that generations to come will know more of Kingdom reality in their lives. I join with their hearts in wanting our ceiling to be your floor!

Read Kevin and Chad's book and believe that as you take daily risks to love radically the one in front of you, the Lord Jesus will use you to change the world!

HEIDI BAKER, PhD
Founding Director, Iris Global

>> INTRODUCTION

Risk is not the only factor needed to step into our supernatural destiny. It may be argued that risk is not the most essential factor needed, but one thing I am certain of: Without the risk factor, we will never step into our supernatural destiny.

As Christians, we are called to do the impossible. We are called to a supernatural destiny. The angel of the Lord encouraged Mary that, *"nothing is impossible for those who believe"* (see Matt. 17:20). As *believers*, then, we are commissioned to live a supernatural lifestyle of risk-taking in order to accomplish the impossible.

Jesus commanded His disciples to *"Preach this message: 'The Kingdom of Heaven is near.' Heal the sick, raise the dead, cleanse those who have leprosy, drive out demons..."* (Matt. 10:7-8). Like the original disciples, we are all called to participate in making disciples of all nations (see Matt. 28:19); employing signs and wonders, healing, and the prophetic; requiring a supernatural empowerment in order to fulfill our call (see Acts 1:8).

Thankfully, we have been given the resources to accomplish this impossible mission. Like Jesus, as described by Peter in Acts 10:38, we have been anointed by the Holy Spirit and with power, and God is with us. On the Day of Pentecost, the Church received the first fruits of the *more* that was to come in the empowering presence of the Holy Spirit. Like the disciples, we have been completely equipped to carry out our commission.

Certainly, being filled with God's Spirit, His presence and power, provides the impetus to step out in our supernatural destiny, but at some point, we must take risk to release what is inside of us. The only way to accomplish our supernatural destiny is by taking risk.

John Wimber taught me that faith is spelled **RISK.**

I developed an acronym using the word *risk,* which will help you as you read through this book.

R—Radical

There is nothing safe about taking risk. It often looks unreasonable and unattainable to onlookers as well as those taking risk.

I—Individual

No one can take risk for us. Each one of us must do it ourselves.

S—Sensible

Risk is a key core value of the Kingdom. Therefore, it makes sense to pursue a lifestyle of risk—it is normal.

K—Kinetic

We cannot just talk about risk—we must set it into motion—we must do it!

Throughout the course of this book, Chad and I will be using the word *risk* to describe faith. These two words are inseparable. Without faith a person cannot take risk, and without risk, there is no faith.

Furthermore, there is a difference between *the Faith* and *having faith.* Throughout the New Testament, *the Faith* is used to describe Christianity (see Matt. 24:10; Acts 6:7; 14:22; 16:5; 1 Cor. 16:13; Gal. 1:23; 6:10; Eph. 4:5,13; Phil. 1:25; Col. 2:7; 1 Tim. 1:2; 3:9; 4:1; 5:8; 6:12-13,21; 2 Tim. 4:7; 1 Pet. 5:9). A person can be in *the Faith,* but not living *by faith.*

I have gone through seasons of my own life in which I have opted for a safer Christian journey. I have found, however, that the only way to step into my supernatural destiny is by continually looking for opportunities to break through the fear barrier and take increasing measures of risk.

Throughout this book, Chad and I will be focusing on various principles that have helped us step across the chicken line and step into our supernatural destiny. This is most certainly a father and son project. In attempting to give unbiased perspectives, we did not read each other's chapters until we had each completed our writing. So then, while we may have used some of the same Scriptures to explain the Risk Factor, we have put our own perspectives to them.

Our desire is that you receive an impartation for greater levels of risk-taking so that, as the apostle Paul prayed, *"...you and I may be mutually encouraged by each other's faith"* (Rom. 1:12). My heart would be that, just as Chad has taken my ceiling and made it his floor, so too, you would take our combined ceiling and make it your floor of equipping, empowerment, and activation.

Finally, our hope is that all of our readers will become world-changers and history makers—revivalists who live in and release the supernatural Kingdom of God in signs and wonders. Our prayer is the same as the apostle Paul's when he prayed, *"I thank my God through Jesus Christ for all of you, because your faith is being reported all over the world"* (Rom. 1:8).

—KEVIN DEDMON

SECTION 1

THE SUPERNATURAL NATURE OF RISK

CHAPTER 1

Kevin Dedmon >> **REVIVAL ROI**

Several years ago, in December, I tore the meniscus in my right knee while playing basketball, causing myself pain whenever I ran or bent my knee under pressure. The options I had at that point were surgery or healing. I had several people pray for miraculous reparation of the meniscus, but there was no improvement. After a month of contending for healing breakthrough, it looked like I was going to have to settle for surgery.

Unfortunately, I had just bought a non-refundable season pass to our local ski area, which left me in a dilemma. I knew that if I had surgery the ski season would be over for me because of the rehabilitation required to recover strength in the knee.

Skiing has been one of my passions since I got my first pair of wooden skis for my tenth Christmas. Since taking off down the "bunny hill" that first winter, I have skied "double black diamond" terrain that is strictly reserved for only the bravest of advanced skiers. I have launched off cliffs and over jagged rock formations and skied head high moguls down steeps that would deter the faint-hearted.

At the beginning of January, the snow on the mountain was perfect. It had been snowing constantly for several days, and the weather forecast for the next day was promising a perfect "bluebird" sunny day. So, I decided that I would make use of my season pass for the first time of the season and see how well I could ski on one and a half legs!

When I arrived at the ski area, I was full of excitement and anticipation with the prospect of skiing for the first time since the end of the previous season. My excitement turned to exasperation, however, when I could barely find the strength in my knee to push down to lock my ski boot into the binding. After 10 minutes of painful determination, soaked with perspiration, I finally locked the binding down; I then proceeded to the chair lift leading to the "green" ski runs designed for beginners.

Even though it was humiliating to ski on such low level runs, I told myself that it would be worth the disgrace just to be in nature on such a beautiful sun-filled day overlooking miles of snow-capped mountains. On the way up the chair lift, I began to feel the adrenaline welling up as I breathed in the fresh mountain air and anticipated an exciting day of skiing on one leg.

The first run was a little tentative as I adjusted to my new style of skiing. By the second run, I was skiing confidently, but knew that I could not handle even a "blue run" because of the uselessness of my right leg. By the third run, I found myself thinking about going home and taking a nap.

Normally, I would ski from opening to closing without even taking a lunch break, but on this day, I found myself feeling tired after only three easy runs. Obviously, I was not tired due to the strenuous demands of the terrain, but because of the boredom. I was bored because there was no real risk in what I was doing. It felt about as adventurous as a slow walk around a cinder oval track. As a result, I did not need any adrenalin and, therefore, felt no energy to continue the monotony.

I immediately chided myself: *What am I thinking? It's a beautiful bluebird day, and I am outside enjoying God's creation!* Even so, I needed more motivation to continue to ski. I needed the Risk Factor. I needed to feel like I could potentially die, or at least be injured, if I made a mistake. Without the possibility of severe consequences, the activity did not justify the effort. So I went home and took a nap.

When I woke up, I scheduled the surgery to repair the meniscus tear. Ironically, the surgery did not turn out well, and I ended up with an infection. After limping around for several weeks with no recovery in sight, I was miraculously healed at a Supernatural Lifestyle conference that I was leading. Thankfully, I am back to skiing "double black diamond" runs, where my adrenal glands get a great workout!

WE WERE CREATED TO TAKE RISK

There is something that moves us when we watch adventure films of people skiing down cliff faces on the verge of death or riding 60-foot mountainous waves that could kill them at any moment. Most of us watch those films with envious admiration, thinking that we would love to have the courage to attempt these death-defying feats.

Living as Christians in the Kingdom of God is the same way. Without some kind of risk, there is little reason for our existence.

There is something inside each one of us that resonates with a desire to take some kind of adventurous action.

As believers, we were designed to live by faith. The apostle Paul points out that, *"The righteous will live by faith"* (Rom. 1:17; Gal. 3:11). In other words, it is normal for Christians to pursue a lifestyle that is characterized by risk.

Now, you may not have the opportunity or the expertise to take on a 60-foot wave or ski down a double black diamond ski run, but at some point, you will have to take some kind of risk in order to step into your supernatural destiny. In fact, there is no way to live *in* the Faith, *by* faith, without taking risk. Without some kind of action, there is no faith. Risk is the expression of faith.

The apostle James describes the correlation between faith and risk in the following passage:

> *What good is it, my brothers, if a man claims to have faith but has no deeds? Can such faith save him? Suppose a brother or sister is without clothes and daily food. If one of you says to him, "Go, I wish you well; keep warm and well fed," but does nothing about his physical needs, what good is it? In the same way, faith by itself, if it is not accompanied by action, is dead. But someone will say, "You have faith; I have deeds." Show me your faith without deeds, and I will show you my faith by what I do. You believe that there is one God. Good! Even the demons believe that—and shudder. You foolish man, do you want evidence that faith without deeds is useless? Was not our ancestor Abraham considered righteous for what he did when he offered his son Isaac on the altar? You see that his faith and his actions*

were working together, and his faith was made complete by what he did. And the scripture was fulfilled that says, "Abraham believed God, and it was credited to him as righteousness," and he was called God's friend. You see that a person is justified by what he does and not by faith alone. In the same way, was not even Rahab the prostitute considered righteous for what she did when she gave lodging to the spies and sent them off in a different direction? As the body without the spirit is dead, so faith without deeds is dead (James 2:14-26).

Risk is the *action* that we take and the *deeds* that we do in response to the level of faith that we have. In other words, without taking some kind of risk, we cannot say we are living in faith. Risk is the evidence that we have faith.

Many people dream about taking risk one day, living in a virtual reality of a potential extreme adventure. Others live vicariously through someone else's risk-taking venture, cheering them on from the safety of the sidelines or the comfort of the couch. Risk is not a spectator sport. Each one of us must personally determine to step out in risk in order to step into our supernatural destiny.

I heard of a high-wire acrobat who connected a cable between two high-rise buildings. A crowd formed 100 feet below as the man took a few steps out onto the cable. The crowd gasped as he began to balance on one leg and then twirl around and do a handstand. Pulling a chair off the rooftop, he then miraculously balanced himself on one leg of a chair. The crowd erupted in a hail of explosive cheers as the acrobat waved down at them with delight.

When the crowd finally quieted down, in anticipation of the next daring feat, he shouted down, "Who believes that I could walk across this cable stretching between these two buildings?" Confidently, they all shouted back that they believed in him. The acrobat responded back to the crowd, "OK, who will be the first to come up here and ride across on my back!" Not one of them took the challenge.

If we are going to step into our supernatural destiny, then at some point, we are going to have to climb to a place beyond our comfort zone, willing to live at uncomfortable heights of risk while balancing on seemingly flimsy foundations of faith.

RISK IS ENTERING THE DANGER ZONE

Webster's Dictionary defines *risk* as "having the possibility of loss or injury." Risk is the potential of impending peril. It is someone or something that creates or suggests a hazard.

As Christians, then, we are only living by faith when we are willing to walk the line, having the potential of losing everything in the process. Jesus said, *"Whoever finds his life will lose it, and whoever loses his life for My sake will find it"* (Matt. 10:39). In other words, if we truly believe in Jesus, we will live a life of risk. Moreover, we cannot say that we are taking risk if there is no potential for some kind of loss or danger.

So then, at some point, as "believers," called to live lives of risk, we must go beyond what we think is possible. We must be willing to lose our security, safety, status, reputation, and respect. In reality, if we are confident that we can accomplish something without the possibility of it going bad or not working out as we had planned, then we have not taken risk. Risk is only evident when we step out of the safety zone to enter into the realm of the seemingly impossible.

Furthermore, as Christians, if we can accomplish something on our own, then we cannot say that we have taken risk. We are called to do the impossible. For example, risk is required to accomplish Jesus' command to heal the sick, raise the dead, cleanse lepers, and cast out evil spirits (see Matt. 10:7-8). We cannot heal anyone or raise someone from the dead. Only the supernatural power of God can provide the means necessary to bring about the desired result.

In each instance in which I have taken risk, resulting in miraculous breakthrough, it was an impossible situation that required absolute faith in God's ability to miraculously intervene. When Peter healed the crippled man at the Gate Beautiful, he said to the crowd, *"Do not look at me as though it was my power or godliness that made this man whole..."* (Acts 3:12). Like Peter, we do not have the power to heal someone, but our risk releases God's power to intervene and accomplish the impossible.

Living as a supernatural Christian requires a partnership of my risk and His power. In this narrative of the miraculous healing of the man at the Gate Beautiful, we are told that it was only after Peter reached down and picked the man up that strength came into the man's feet and ankles, enabling him to walk (see Acts 3:7). Peter took risk, and God supplied the supernatural power to bring about the miracle.

Amazingly, I have seen the impossible come about on many occasions when I have stepped out in taking risk. Conversely, I have rarely seen intervention for impossible supernatural breakthrough when I have refrained from taking risk. The supernatural is released through risk.

Recently, I was speaking at a conference with about 500 people in attendance. Just as I was introduced, I had a thought that God wanted to heal people who had metal in their bodies. This was a huge point of risk for me because I had never specifically selected these types of conditions to focus on for healing.

For a moment, as I stood facing the crowd, I felt like I was getting ready to paddle into a 60-foot mountainous wave. I thought, *What am I thinking? This is over my head!* Immediately, however, I heard myself asking for people with metal in their bodies to stand. I had just entered the danger zone, and I was past the point of no return.

Amazingly, metal began dissolving in people's bodies throughout the auditorium! Dozens of people began shouting out that the metal in their backs, necks, and extremities had dissolved and that they could move freely without pain. Approximately 75 people had the metal in their bodies dissolve in a five-minute window because I stepped out of my comfort zone and took risk to do the impossible!

RISK RELEASES ROI

Leo Buscaglia, the popular professor at the University of Southern California, as well as best-selling author and international motivational speaker, emphasized:

> The person who risks nothing, does nothing, has nothing, is nothing, and becomes nothing. He may avoid suffering and sorrow, but he simply cannot learn and feel and change and grow and love and live.[1]

The only way to step into our supernatural destiny is to take some kind of risk. Risk is like an investment.

For most of us, when we approach a potential investment, we consider the risk and then weigh it against the potential return on investment—*ROI*. Often, the *ROI* is commensurate to the level of risk; the higher the level of risk, the greater potential for a high return. Therefore, the very fact that an activity carries a certain amount of risk reveals that the potential return on that risk may be well worth the investment.

As Christians, when we invest what God has given us, He promises that the return on that investment (ROI) will be rewarded with increase. In the parable of the talents, Jesus makes the point that if we take risk to invest what we have been given, then more will be added to us (see Matt. 25:14-30). In other words, in the Kingdom we get a great return on investment (ROI) when we take risk.

Moreover, we cannot get a return on something we do not invest in. In other words: No risk, no reward. Like the fearful servant who took his one talent and hid it, we will not only miss out on our supernatural destiny, but will also lose everything we have held on to in fear. Importantly, the confidence we have in God's promises to provide for us will determine the amount of risk we take in putting everything on the line.

I once met a former professional gambler who likened faith to gambling. He said, "It's like getting an inside tip on a horse, taking everything you own to the track, going to the betting window, and putting everything on that horse." Ironically, when he received Christ into his life, he was so filled with faith that he took risk to go back to the people he had stolen from and scammed to support his addiction, and he made things right!

Risk is the action that we take in response to the level of faith we have. In Hebrews 11:1, faith is defined as, *"being sure of what we hope for and certain of what we do not see."* When we are confident in God's promises, we are more likely to take risk.

In Revelation 22:12, Jesus promised, *"Behold, I am coming soon! My reward is with Me, and I will give to everyone according to what he has done."* When we invest in the things of the Kingdom, our reward will be great. It is a sure bet to take risk in doing the things Jesus has asked each of us to accomplish.

The apostle Paul was counting on a good ROI when, at the end of his life, he said,

> *I have fought the good fight, I have finished the race, I have kept the faith. Now there is in store for me the crown of righteousness, which the Lord, the righteous Judge, will award to me on that day—and not only to me, but also to all who have longed for His appearing* (2 Timothy 4:7-8).

I believe keeping the faith is contingent upon keeping our eye on the reward. When I am confident that God comes through with His supernatural resources as I step out in a lifestyle of risk, I find myself making continual investments.

I often will take risk to release healing on people when I am out in the community, going about my day. Each time I step out, however, I find myself going through an analysis process that goes something like this: *I'm going to look foolish and incompetent if they do not get healed!* Then I'll remember all of the miracles I have seen when I took risk in the past, and I'll conclude: *OK, I'll take the risk—It is worth the potential embarrassment, in order to obtain the reward of seeing people healed.*

When we take risk to release the supernatural Kingdom of God, we open up the possibility for the miraculous. Risk is an investment of faith that releases the supernatural Kingdom of God in our lives and circumstances.

Most people do not take risk because they lack confidence that God will come through on His end of the partnership and intervene in our risk-taking efforts. As believers, it is essential that we understand that God is faithful; when we take risk, He comes.

The last part of Hebrews 11:6 promises that, "He rewards those who earnestly seek Him." This statement is placed in the context of demonstrating faith in God's promises. In order to take risk, we must have confidence that God is going to come through for us.

The Heroes of the Faith are listed in Hebrews chapter 11 as those who took unreasonable risk. Certainly, they had assessed the potential downside to their risk venture, but in their analysis, the reward for holding onto their promise outweighed the potential fall-out of failure. They made way for the impossible because they invested in the promise with acts of risk.

Abraham is a classic example of one who focused on the reward of his risk. The writer to the Hebrews tells us that,

> By faith Abraham, even though he was past age—and Sarah herself was barren—was enabled to become a father because he considered Him faithful who had made the promise. And so from this one man, and he as good as dead, came descendants as numerous as the stars in the sky and as countless as the sand on the seashore (Hebrews 11:11-12).

If we truly believe God is able to do the impossible then, like Abraham, we will determine to ride upon the prophetic promises that God has given us to carry out. We will live in the hope that God is faithful to provide what we need to bring about the promise that our risk is releasing. We can only enter into our God-given supernatural destiny as we step out in risk.

RISK RELEASES BREAKTHROUGH

Risk is the spark that ignites the fire of God's passion to be released in and through our lives. Jesus said,

...I tell you the truth, if you have faith as small as a mustard seed, you can say to this mountain, "Move from here to there" and it will move. Nothing will be impossible for you (Matthew 17:20).

Like an out-of-control wild fire that is ignited by a tiny strike of a match, so too, miraculous breakthrough is ignited by even the smallest level of risk.

Before He ascended into Heaven, Jesus promised,

> *And these signs will accompany those who believe: In My name they will drive out demons; they will speak in new tongues; they will pick up snakes with their hands; and when they drink deadly poison, it will not hurt them at all; they will place their hands on sick people, and they will get well* (Mark 16:17-18).

When we take risk—when we believe—we open the door that allows God's supernatural power to break into our circumstances. Risk is like opening a door to a closed up building in which a fire has been raging, creating a "back draft" explosion of pent up power. Our risk releases God's power into the environment.

I'll never forget an experience I had while leading a mission team of about 30 of our School of Supernatural Ministry students to Ecuador. Our team was invited to minister in the intensive care unit at a children's hospital. Upon arriving, we were informed that there were 15 separate intensive care wards with approximately 30 children in each ward. In order to minister to each critically ill child, we decided to separate into teams of three, including a translator.

As my team worked our way around the intensive care unit we were assigned to, we saw many of the children, and most of the parents who where there, experience amazing supernatural healing breakthrough. Along with healing prayer, we then prophesied to each one about the good plans and purposes God had for them. Amazingly, several of them asked Jesus into their hearts, and others rededicated their lives to the Lord.

About 45 minutes into this time, I felt like I had a word of knowledge for a nurse who had a hurt left foot. Taking the translator with me, I approached the nurses' station and asked if any of them had a hurt left foot. All eight of them looked at me with blank expressions, indicating that none of them had a problem with their left foot. I asked again, looking at each one of them as though they may not have heard me the first time. They all shook their heads, no.

I responded to the group of nurses, now gazing at me as though they were deer in the headlights, "Are you sure you don't have a problem with your left foot because I really felt like God wanted to heal someone's left foot?" They each assured me that they would know whether or not they had a problem with their left foot, giving me a look that communicated, "Leave us alone."

So I went back to the patients and began ministering to one of the young girls and her parents. About five minutes later, as I was preparing the girl for healing, I could feel a presence behind me. I looked over my shoulder to find three nurses standing behind me with their arms crossed.

My initial thought was, *Oh great, these nurses think I am a kook, and they are going to ask me to leave the hospital.* I asked through the translator whether they could wait a few minutes while I finished helping this girl and her parents. They nodded, yes, and I thought to myself, *Well, at least I'll get to minister to one more patient before being kicked out!*

A few minutes later, after ministering to the girl, I turned to the nurses, asking them how I could help them. The first nurse explained that none of them had a hurt left foot, but that she had a torn rotator cuff. She went on to explain that she had just seen the doctor overseeing the intensive care ward, and his advice was to have surgery, and he told her that she should not continue to work because of her inability to lift her patients.

The second nurse had just informed the first nurse that she had the flu and was going to have to go home, leaving the intensive care unit understaffed. I forget the third nurse's ailment, but all three were instantly healed and went straight back to work!

About five minutes later, the first nurse, who had just been healed, came back to ask if I would come to the nurses' station. When I arrived, there were a dozen or so nurses from nearby stations gathered around needing healing for various ailments. All of them were instantly healed, and before long, nurses from all over the hospital were lined out the door because they had heard about their co-workers being healed.

The scene looked like a raucous New Year's Eve party as the healed nurses expressed their excitement. Many of them received Jesus and were filled with the Holy Spirit, laughing uncontrollably!

One nurse, who had just been healed, stood against the wall, laughing and confessing that she felt like she was drunk! She later went home and convinced her son and his girlfriend to attend our evening meeting at the local church. They came, and both were healed and asked Jesus into their hearts that night!

All of this came about over a wrong word of knowledge. When we take risk, God explodes onto the scene. In reality, it is not our performance that brings breakthrough of the supernatural—it is simply our simple and sometimes silly-looking risk.

THE PURPOSE OF FAITH

In Hebrews 11:6, we are told that, *"without faith, it is impossible to please God...."* Notice, that it is not our performance or success that pleases God. Rather, it is faith expressed in risk that pleases God. Even when we take risk and give a wrong word of knowledge, God is pleased.

In this venture of stepping out in risk, it is important to note that our intrinsic value and position as His children are not greater—He is already fully pleased with us. The Father was already pleased with Jesus before He took risk to pray for someone, walk on water, or turn water into wine.

At Jesus' baptism, the Father said, *"This is My Son, whom I love, and with Him I am well pleased"* (Matt. 3:17). In the same way, God is already pleased with us because we are His children. We cannot do one thing to get any more of His pleasure toward us.

Rather, God is pleased with the fact that our risk-taking affords Him the opportunity to intervene in our lives and circumstances. He is pleased because He gets to do something! God is waiting for us to pursue the impossible so that He can work on our behalf. In a sense, we relieve God, and the angels of Heaven, from boredom when we take risk.

In God's sovereignty, He has determined that He will speak through us and work through our hands here on the earth. As

Christ's ambassadors, we are His mouthpieces, and we are His hands extended. Certainly, it is *"Christ in us, the hope of glory,"* but the Christ in us is just waiting to be the Christ through us, to become the hope of glory for others around us. He wants to intervene in people's lives, and it is our risk that unties His hands and unleashes His voice to release the miraculous that we so desperately need.

The apostle James promises that, *"The prayer offered in faith will make the sick person well; the Lord will raise him up..."* (James 5:14-15). God is just waiting for us to trust that He will intervene in our lives. Risk is the action that proves that we truly believe.

In the parable of the persistent widow, Jesus concludes with the question, *"...When the Son of Man comes, will He find faith on the earth?"* (Luke 18:8). In other words, will we be among those who keep taking risk until Jesus returns? Risk is not to be just a one-time event, but a lifestyle. The apostle Paul exhorts, *"Examine yourselves to see whether you are in the faith; test yourselves. Do you not realize that Christ Jesus is in you...?"* (2 Cor. 13:5).

How long has it been since you have stepped out in risk? What is holding you back from making huge investments of supernatural ventures? What is preventing you from going after the impossible dreams?

I want to encourage you that as you apply the risk factor and step into your supernatural destiny, God will empower you to go to the next levels of supernatural breakthrough. I release an impartation of grace to live a radical lifestyle of radical risk!

ENDNOTE

1. Leo F. Buscaglia, quoted at Thinkexist.com; http://thinkexist .com/quotation/the_person_who_risks_nothing-does _nothing-has/148405.html; accessed September 8, 2011.

CHAPTER 2

Chad Dedmon ➤➤ LIVING THE LIFE

As I tiptoed to look over the edge of the bridge to see where I was going to be landing, my heart started pounding loudly in my throat. I peered over the edge and saw a wide expanse of canyon with a rushing river at the bottom. The attendant promptly informed me that my head might touch the water when I got to the bottom, 150 feet below, but to just relax and jump, and the bungee would take care of the rest. I thought to myself, *Easy for him to say. This seems illogical—it's not like the bridge is collapsing or there is an earthquake. I am actually paying someone to assist me in jumping off a bridge with only a bungee cord tied around my legs. I am putting myself at risk to die here.* My mind was racing with thoughts like: The bungee could snap; this jump could lead to my death.

My wife and I had just arrived in Queenstown, New Zealand, the adventure capital of the world—the last leg of our journey. One year earlier, we had decided to quit our jobs and the security of a paycheck and follow God's leading into the nations of the world. It was there in Queenstown that I learned a saying from the local New Zealanders that says, "Go big or go home!" So, of course, I had to go big and try bungee jumping in the place where it originated.

My wife was at the bottom with a video camera in hand, screaming words of encouragement. As I was walking over to the edge, I looked behind me to see a 73-year-old woman waiting to jump after me. She looked very scared and was talking about pulling out from the jump. I gave her a nervous smile and I said, "If I do it first and don't die, will you promise to jump after me?" She thought for a second and said, "OK, you look a bit heavier than I do so if the cord holds you, it will definitely hold me."

In an effort to muster up all the courage I had, I forced myself to walk to the edge of the bridge. I had a lot of fear intensifying inside of me, but suddenly had a moment of mental clarity. The thought came to me: *People have been jumping off this bridge for decades and no one has yet fallen to their death.* If they could do it, I could do it! I could feel a surge of adrenaline running through my veins, and I quickly jumped out as far as I could possibly go, accompanied with the loudest shout I could let out!

That three-second free fall was one of the most exhilarating moments of my life, and it came from taking one of the biggest death-defying risks I have ever taken. Similarly, when we are taking risk in the supernatural, we will have to confront and overcome intimidation and fear by choosing to walk past them into faith. That same feeling of fear and hesitation mixed with excitement and adrenaline is what we will always experience before taking a jump and taking risk in the supernatural. Faith cannot be a feeling; it is rather a decision in which we choose to jump!

We are invited by a supernatural God every day to step out to the edge of the bridge and jump in the realm of the Spirit into the unknown. Fortunately, the best news about taking risks is that it is fun. I can tell you from firsthand experience that new parts of your heart will come alive when you activate your faith. This could look like prophesying over a stranger while shopping or giving a word of knowledge to your neighbor in passing. The reward of risk, then, is to see people getting touched by the revelation that God is personal and cares about their daily lives.

Moreover, we are not designed to take risk only once in a great while. One of the pitfalls of taking great risk is that we can camp in yesterday's victory rather than having the mindset of perpetually pioneering new frontiers. As we take more ground, we need to be thankful for the breakthrough that we see. However, it is vital that we fight off complacency instead of settling for the level of faith that we have operated from in the past. In order for our spirits to remain healthy and prosperous, we have to constantly live in the faith realm so that we can be sustained with fresh nutrients from Heaven. We will become malnourished if we only eat yesterday's bread!

In Matthew 4:4, Jesus declares to the enemy when facing temptation that *"man does not live from bread alone but from every word* [rhema] *that proceeds from the mouth of God."* As we listen for the Word of the Lord, we will be leaning into His voice and getting new strategies for victory. Each time we break through in the realm of faith, it releases fresh manna for us in the realm of the Spirit. We can't live in yesterday's breakthrough or, like the Israelites found out in Exodus, our faith will turn into moldy bread! We need fresh bread from Heaven every day. When we take risk and exercise our faith, we will begin to see the heart of our heavenly Father manifested in new ways.

Our Father is inviting us to step into the unknown. He is asking us to be courageous and to jump over the edge with Him into a lifestyle of adventure. When we do, we will realize that we were born to be in constant communion and fellowship with the Holy Spirit. When this happens, we will begin to walk in step with the rhythms of His heart.

As Christ-followers, we are called to operate in supernatural faith. In our daily lives, it is possible to partner with the Kingdom of Heaven to release the Holy Spirit into the atmosphere around us. Living in a lifestyle of risk activates the faith realm and unlocks natural impossibilities.

While I was at Bethel Church in Redding, California, I had an open vision in which I saw Heaven invading Earth. In the vision, there were buses and cars going back and forth from Earth to Heaven. People were jumping on the buses and handing money to the drivers. I reached into my pocket to see if I had any money to ride the bus because I also wanted to go. I pulled out several bills that had the word *faith* written on the bills.

Instantly, I had the revelation that faith is the currency of Heaven. As I got on the bus, I was pulled into Heaven and saw a line of shops along the street (similar to what they look like here on Earth). In these shops, you could buy brand new body parts for people that were in need of a miracle. I saw a knee available and decided to buy that. I pulled out the faith bills from my pocket and exchanged them for a knee. When I stepped back onto the bus, I immediately came out of the encounter, and was back sitting in my chair at Bethel Church in Redding, California.

Right away, I knew I must give a word of knowledge for anyone with knee problems. Eight people responded, and I began to pray for their knees. As I laid my hands on them, they began to feel heat and all the pain leaving! There was a man in this same group who had a large knee brace and was going in for surgery because of torn knee ligaments. After prayer, on his own initiative, he tore off his knee brace and started jumping around and performing leg squats. He was completely astonished and extremely happy that God had just touched and healed his knee.

After this experience, I began to have a whole new understanding that faith is the currency of Heaven. Faith accesses the miraculous and overcomes impossibilities, bringing what is in Heaven to Earth in a tangible form.

In Hebrews, we learn that faith is the substance of the things that are unseen (see Heb. 11:1). Faith is actually a substance, and it is recognizable. Believing and having great faith make Heaven a reality here on Earth.

We are mandated to represent Jesus to a world that is longing for an encounter with a loving and personal God. I have often heard Bill Johnson say, "We owe the world an authentic encounter with Jesus." Therefore, the greatest message we can give the world will not be a sermon, but living our lives out with great faith for all those around us to witness. If faith is a substance (matter, material, stuff), then there must be a way to set it in motion so it can be released and given away. There are numerous examples of how faith can be released and manifested in and through our lives.

The essence of faith cannot be exemplified by words alone, but through action. In First Corinthians 2:4-5, Paul writes,

My message and my preaching were not with wise and persuasive words, but with a demonstration of the Spirit's power, so that your faith should not rest on men's wisdom, but on God's power.

Paul communicates here that our faith should rest on the power of God more than on eloquent speech and doctrinal arguments.

If there was anyone who could preach a great message, it was the apostle Paul. Paul's lifelong and scholarly study of the Scriptures made him an expert in dissecting every aspect of the Law. However, he discovered that the most effective way to "re-present" the Gospel was through displaying the *dunamis* power of God. We are called to display the Gospel in our everyday lives, rather than just use our words. I have found that seeing people healed of diseases or pain in their bodies is much better than any message I have ever preached.

One of the church fathers that came out of the Jesus People movement in the 1970s was John Wimber. He coined the phrase that faith is spelled R-I-S-K. Although I only needed to draw upon my bravery once to bungee jump off of a bridge, it was an event that built up my courage. However, normal Christianity is living in faith and taking risk every day; it cannot just be a one-time event.

There are days when I take greater risk than others. I may not need to take a high-level risk like bungee jumping every day. However, we are called to steward the measure of faith that we have cultivated throughout our lives. It is essential that we draw upon the equity of our faith every day. Our faith should not lie dormant in us; it must be activated and demonstrated. We are called to live out of our comfort zone and in the faith realm, where we access Heaven and reveal God's goodness to those around us.

When we receive Christ into our hearts, we are transformed into His image and likeness. We will begin to manifest the qualities of Christ and the Spirit of Jesus through our lives. Luke 9:1 tells us, *"When Jesus had called the Twelve together, he gave them power and author-ity to drive out all demons and to cure diseases."* The word *power* in the

Greek translation here is *dunamis*. According to *Strong's Greek Lexicon*, *dunamis* means "force, miraculous power, ability, might, abundance, worker of miracles, power, strength, and mighty wonderful work."[1]

We are called to move in this same *dunamis* power as Jesus did and display His glory and love here on the Earth. When Jesus commissioned us to do the same works He does, He gave a fresh impartation of grace for every believer to fulfill His words. This grace is not just for the "special ones" or those that have been called to "full-time ministry." We, as co-heirs, are all receiving the same grace that Jesus possessed!

I have discovered that grace releases a supernatural ability to step into our destiny. Colossians 2:9 states,

> *For in Christ, all the fullness of the deity lives in bodily form and you have been given fullness in Christ who is the head over every power and authority.*

We have received the fullness of Christ living inside of us; therefore, there is no lack for us in Him. It is not by our own merit, but by His grace, that we are filled.

We can, therefore, no longer give the excuse, "I don't have what it takes," because of the person living inside of us—we have been given the fullness of Christ! If we are going to walk in the greater works (see John 14:12), we need to operate from the fullness of what we already possess and be aware of what is available to us.

Another place where God tells us that we have been given every blessing is in Ephesians 1:3, *"Praise be to the God and Father of our Lord Jesus Christ who has blessed us in the heavenly realms with every spiritual blessing in Christ."* In this Scripture, he was not talking to generals of the faith, but to every believer. Here again, Paul communicates to us that we already possess every spiritual blessing. Jesus understood that it was His Father's pleasure to give Him the Kingdom of Heaven. He had every resource at His disposal.

Like Jesus, we are called to be ambassadors (or representatives) of Heaven and, therefore, have the right to inherit and possess those blessings. We are grafted in as sons and daughters through the bloodline of Jesus; therefore, we get to access all of Heaven's resources. Each day, as we go into our workplaces and interact within our communities, we can function out of this extravagant blessing of grace and oneness with Jesus. We draw upon the account of Heaven as we take risk, activating our faith, and then see Heaven invade Earth.

Jesus' life was not consumed with miracle services, crusades, and conferences. Rather, He simply lived His life, displaying the nature of the Father everywhere He went. Jesus said things like, *"When you have seen me, you have seen the Father"* (see John 14:9) and *"I and my Father are one"* (John 10:30). People followed Him because they knew He was connected with the Life Source.

Jesus was only able to meet the needs of the people because He spent time with His Father and continued to always lean in to hear the voice of His Dad. From this place of confidence, He confronted every place of sickness, poverty, and darkness in the humanity around Him. He was not affected or swayed by the present earthly realm. He lived in the faith realm where anything is possible, making Heaven a present reality while He lived on Earth.

I have learned that I have a green light wherever I go to release the Kingdom of Heaven anywhere. People often ask the question, "Should I wait for the healing anointing to come or feel a Holy Spirit unction before I approach someone to ask them if they want to receive prayer?" Certainly, I have a high value for the anointing and leading of the Spirit through discerning His voice, but there are times when I feel no electricity, don't have any promptings or impressions, and do not get a word of knowledge. Basically, if I see someone limping or in pain or in a cast, crutches, or wheelchair—without any further inspiration from the Holy Spirit—I believe it is my responsibility to approach them and ask if they would like to be healed.

I remember Bill Johnson telling us about a visitor who came to Redding and asked, "When is the mall outreach?" Bill began to think through all the outreaches that happen in the weekly life at Bethel Church. After a quick mental checklist of all the outreaches, he explained to the visitor that there was no mall outreach. The visitor insisted there had to be one because he had heard a story shared about some people from Bethel Church who went into the mall and saw healings occur. Bill remembered the story and told them that there wasn't a mall outreach; rather, we just have people in our church who like to shop! When living in a place of risk, it becomes normal to shop and stop to pray for people while you are doing life.

I love to take risk in restaurants and grocery stores, and I have seen so many people healed and touched by God in different places of business. People sometimes ask me, "Is it weird to just be hanging out in grocery stores and be looking around for people to pray for?" I laugh and tell them that I am in the grocery store most of the time not because I got a word of knowledge, but because I am just shopping for food.

Several years ago, when my wife and I were first married, we both worked at restaurants. One night, specifically, I was finished earlier than my wife, and like any other 23-year-old, I was hungry. During these years, it was normal for me to have two dinners, one before work and one after. One of my favorite foods is donuts, so I set out to go to the grocery store and get some donuts and milk.

When I arrived at the store, I walked past the checkout aisle, and my attention was drawn toward a woman who had hearing aids in her ears. I approached her and inquired, "How long have you had hearing problems?" She said, "I've had hearing problems since I was a little girl. I have been 90 percent deaf in my left ear and 85 percent deaf in my right ear for over 30 years."

I knew I had a green light and politely asked if I could pray for her. She looked at me nervously, grabbed her groceries, started to walk away and said, "Sure that would be nice." I quickly responded, "I would like to pray for you now, not later at my church or somewhere else, because God wants to heal you right now. Would that be OK? It is only going to take a couple seconds." Looking surprised and a little out of her comfort zone, she put down her groceries and agreed. I asked her if I could place my hands on her ears and if she could take out her hearing aids so that we could tell when God opened up her ears.

It is one of my core values that I honor those in my community when I minister to them. I want them to feel safe and valued, and that's why I will always ask questions and permission from them before I pray. I believe the lady at the grocery store felt very valued because I had specifically asked to pray for her right then after I waited for her agreement.

I laid my hands on her ears while she held her hearing aids in her hand. During this whole time, the checkout clerk had been listening to and watching our conversation and prayer time. She seemed to be in her early 20s and was very curious to see what was going to take place.

After I said a short prayer, Jesus opened up the lady's ears. I immediately tested out her hearing by whispering my name in her ear. I then backed up and told her to repeat what I was saying. Amazingly, I was 30 feet away, and the lady was repeating verbatim everything I was saying. Shocked, the young checkout clerk looked at me and said, "I can't hear you!" Suddenly, all three of us realized that the older woman who had hearing loss could hear better than the young checkout clerk.

Both women had tears in their eyes as they realized that God had healed this woman of hearing loss! As I was thanking God and celebrating with them, I suddenly felt a wind on the back of my neck, and I saw two healing angels flying over me.

Afterward, I knew that God wanted to heal more people in the grocery store because I was immediately impressed with many words of knowledge. This process I went through might sound foreign or strange to you. However, discerning the voice of God can come naturally as we come to understand that our bodies are a temple and that we were made to feel and discern the presence of God.

Hebrews 5:14 says, *"But solid food is for the mature, who by constant use have trained themselves to distinguish good from evil."* For example, when my wife begins to feel tingling up and down her left leg, it is an indicator that the Holy Spirit is speaking to her to prophesy. This manifestation experience has happened at church, in restaurants, and on airplanes. We can feel these indicators from the Holy Spirit at any time or moment, but we must be aware enough to respond when they happen. For me, when I feel wind on the back of my neck, I know that there is a healing angel being activated to heal those around me.

Just after I received the words of knowledge, I walked over to the checkout clerk and said, "I couldn't have done this on my own. What just happened was God!" She nodded her head in agreement that what she had just seen occur was a supernatural encounter with God. I explained that I felt like God wanted to heal more people in the grocery store and noticed the intercom microphone next to her. So, I asked her if I could use the store PA system to notify the people in the store that God wanted to heal them. She told me yes and then showed me how to use it.

I grabbed the store intercom and said, "Attention all shoppers… God is in the building! He has just healed a lady of deafness."

I then had the lady who had been healed quickly share what had happened to her over the intercom. Then I began to share how God wanted to heal many more people in the grocery store. I announced the words of knowledge that I had received, including pain in the wrist, hip, headaches, and stomach pain. I invited those that wanted to be healed to come to checkout station 10 and went over and waited.

After a few minutes, a small group began to gather around the checkout station. A lady in a motorized cart approached me, and asked, "Do you really think God can heal me? I am going in for a hip replacement surgery in a few weeks." I said, "Of course God can heal you because He is the Healer and that is His Name. He can't deny who He is!"

I turned to the lady who had been healed and asked her if she could help me pray for the lady in the motorized cart. I quickly explained that when we receive the Kingdom, we also have the opportunity to give away the Kingdom. I told her that Jesus says in Matthew 10:7-8, *"As you go, preach this message: 'The kingdom of heaven is near.' Heal the sick, raise the dead, cure those with leprosy, and cast out demons. Give as freely as you have received!"*. I explained that when God healed her ears, she received the Kingdom of Heaven. "Since you have been healed," I told her, "it is time to give it away by praying with me for this woman in the motorized cart." She agreed, and we both laid hands on and prayed healing for the woman with the hip problems.

I asked the woman on the motorized cart to test out her hip by moving her leg to see if there was any improvement. She gasped loudly and said, "I couldn't do this before without pain!" Excitedly,

I asked her to try to do something else that she couldn't have done before! Immediately, she got up out of her motorized cart and began walking around to test out her hips. She broke out into a jog, all the while screaming, "Jesus has just healed me!" The people that gathered around witnessed this miracle and were shocked over this wonderful display of God's power.

Out of the corner of my eye, I saw a man pushing his way through to the front. He was shaking his fists at me in a very intense and animated fashion. At first, I thought he might have been upset at me, but instead, he explained that he was a music teacher and made his living by performing and teaching music. He explained that he was experiencing carpel tunnel in both wrists and had been in severe pain for the last two years. He then pleaded for prayer so that he would be healed.

I laid my hands on his wrists and began to pray for him. As soon as I invited God's presence to come, he exclaimed, "My wrists are on fire! They are really hot!" I explained to him that the heat was a good thing and that his wrists were hot because when the Holy Spirit comes and touches us, sometimes a tangible heat begins to penetrate into the place on the body that needs healing. I continued praying for more fire, heat, and healing in his wrists. I asked him to move his wrists in a circular motion and explained that doing this would activate a greater level of healing in his body.

Often, we can help accelerate people's healings by asking them to participate in the process. For example, the lame man who Peter and John prayed for at the city gate was healed while in the action of getting up from his mat and standing with Peter and John (see Acts 3:7). Peter took the lame man by the right hand and lifted him up. As he stood up, his feet and legs received strength.

Amazingly, after the man with carpel tunnel moved his hands in circles, he announced, "All the pain is gone! I could not do this before without pain!" He went on to say that when he walked into the grocery store, he thought to himself, *Wouldn't it be great if all the pain left tonight?* Miraculously, that is exactly what ended up happening.

All of a sudden it dawned on me that the Kingdom had just manifested around me in the grocery store and that it would probably be a good idea to introduce the King! I began to share that Jesus died on the cross so that they could be healed, saved, and set free. Furthermore, He also died in order to pay for our sins and invite us into a deep and personal relationship with Him. I then asked how many of them would like to be best friends with the Creator of the universe? Hands began to go up, and I led them through a prayer to receive Jesus into their hearts as their Lord and Savior.

I began to minister one-on-one to people as they received Jesus, and many people were healed, touched, and saved in that moment. When I got home, I realized that in all the excitement, I had forgotten to buy my donuts! However, forgetting my donuts was well worth seeing God show up in the grocery store, and I was on cloud nine for several weeks afterward.

I believe people want to know Jesus' love personally. They want to know how He can meet them and change and improve their lives at that moment. I have found that once people know He is real, they cannot resist Him!

This story of God breaking in and touching many people in the grocery store is inspiring, but this breakthrough is backed up by a lifestyle of risk that has been stewarded over the years. I don't see this level of healing every time I go into the grocery store, but it is normal for me to pray for people while I go about my day.

I believe the secret to having extreme outbreaks of healing is to faithfully pray for the one God puts in front of you. When I saw the lady in the store who had hearing aids, I recognized in that moment that God had put her right in front of me to minister to. So, when I stepped out and took the risk to pray, the rest of the breakthrough happened.

In the church, we sometimes have a tendency to focus on the crazy outbreaks of miracles and not celebrate those who see headaches healed in their everyday lives. It is essential that we learn to celebrate every breakthrough that God manifests in our midst—even the seemingly small ones.

The journey into the supernatural always begins with obedience in the pursuit of a lifestyle of risk. The crazy outbreaks happen when you are obedient and find "the one" God is asking you to pray for. Jesus told His disciples to *"And as you go, preach, saying, 'The kingdom of heaven is at hand.'"* (Matt. 10:7 NASB). This was not a commissioning for a one-time event. We need to remember the first part of this commissioning is *go!* Everywhere I go, I need to be obedient to bring the message of Heaven to Earth. It is not through words that I live this message out, but by activating my faith.

It is also important to have a thankful heart when seeing breakthrough after stepping out to pray for healing, whether it's a headache healed or a creative miracle performed. People have asked me before how I can get so excited about a headache being healed. I simply tell them that the God of the miraculous just showed up, and we have just had the opportunity to watch Him touch a person's life! Every single healing and miracle brings God glory, whether it is considered to be a big or a small breakthrough.

Finally, it is important that as a community of believers we become intentional about sharing Jesus with others and inspiring one another to go for it. While keeping this in mind, remember that evangelism was not meant to be an event that we put on our calendar once a week. That is only one dimension of evangelism. When we said yes to Jesus and the Holy Spirit came to dwell within us, we became enrolled in the school of the Holy Spirit.

For example, early on when I was learning how to cultivate a life of risk, I realized that I had not prayed for anybody in the marketplace for several weeks. I felt an urgency in my spirit that I needed to get out to pray for some people. I asked God who I should call to come out with me that day and join me in praying. The Holy Spirit told me, "Don't call anyone. Why don't we just go together?" God began to tell me that I am never alone when I go out and do evangelism. Moreover, there are thousands of angels waiting to release healing or bring breakthrough of all kinds, and they partner with us when we step out to take risk.

So, as I went out to a nearby parking lot to pray for people, I had an overwhelming sense of comfort that all of Heaven was backing me up. That is what we all must remember when we go out—that God is always there in our midst. In Hebrews 13:5, the Father releases a promise and tells us that He will never leave us or forsake us. Most Christians take this Scripture and apply it in times of need or trial. However, this Scripture can be functional in every aspect of our lives.

When we understand this truth and start to daily live it out, the fears we thought we had about stepping out into new things dissipate because we know He is with us. When He is for us, who can be against us?

ENDNOTE

1. *Strong's Greek Lexicon*, #1411; http://www.studylight.org/lex /grk/frequency.cgi?number=1411&book=lu&translation= str; accessed September 8, 2011.

SECTION 2

CULTIVATING A SUPERNATURAL CULTURE OF RISK

CHAPTER 3

Kevin Dedmon ▶▶ **I TRIPLE DOG DARE YOU**

I love to play golf. I think it is because golf has so many parallels to real life. As I write this, I am in New Zealand and have just finished playing a round of golf with a local Kiwi. Walking the amazing landscape, we discussed the many life principles that we have learned chasing a little white ball from tee to green, while sometimes taking detours through unimaginable terrain.

After a wayward fading drive on a particular par four, I found myself in a peculiar predicament nestled in the trees ("in jail") with only a very small opening in which to advance my golf ball to the green. My Kiwi playing partner advised me to "punch out" to safety by hitting my golf ball back out onto the paralleling fairway a few yards directly to my left, sucking up to what would amount to be a penalty stroke.

Evaluating the options, I realized that it would take a once-in-a-lifetime effort to make it through the small opening among the trees. If I could pull off the miraculous shot, however, the risk would result in high-fives from my playing partner, as well as a great memory in my personal golf lore. If I missed, I could find myself in an even worse position, resulting in losing even more strokes or maybe even losing my ball once it ricocheted off the many trees. I went for it.

Amazingly, the ball went right through the opening, and landed gently on the green, about ten feet from the hole for a birdie opportunity. It was a miraculous shot. Unfortunately, I missed the putt.

Taking risk is a mind-set; it is a culture—an inner attitude. I have always tried to live my life on the edge, taking risk when there only seemed to be a small opening to reach my supernatural destiny. I can honestly say that I have made it through many openings and have made many putts along the way through life as I have taken risk. Conversely, I have often made triple boogey, as my golf ball has careened off of tree limbs, leaving me in worse shape than when I started—that is risk.

My Kiwi playing partner's philosophy was to always play it safe. His experience had taught him that the safe play worked out more than the spectacular. He was a very good golfer; in fact, he scored better than me that day, but I'm sure I had more fun!

As we discussed our differing playing styles, I explained that my philosophy was to live at a level of danger, adventure, and uncertainty that could lead to extreme miraculous breakthroughs. I went on to say that while the safe shot may pan out and present more opportunity for a par, it would not provide the table talk that would lead to reminiscing about the impossible that was accomplished because of a calculated measure of risk that went beyond reason. I concluded that I do not like triple bogeys, but that I do like amazing, spectacular shots that can lead to birdies. In the same way, the only way to get the miraculous is by taking risk!

In cultivating a supernatural culture of risk, we must be willing to try for the impossible even though we may miss the putt. We must be willing to make our situation worse, in going after our supernatural destiny. In developing a lifestyle of risk, it is important to go for the small openings in life. We may not make every shot, but if we do not try for the miraculous, we will never hit the green of our supernatural destiny.

For the Christian, risk is intended not as a one-time event, but rather, a culture. We cannot say to ourselves, "OK, I stepped out in risk. I'm glad I got that requirement out of the way. Now I can go back to a safe life." No, risk is meant to be a Kingdom lifestyle that is cultivated over time. Risk is only good for the one time it is used. Moreover, taking risk does not come naturally, but must be intentionally pursued as a first option. A lifestyle of risk requires a commitment to continually pursue the impossible.

I consider myself to be a risk-taker, but every time I take risk, my heart is beating as though it were the first time stepping into the impossible. I never get used to taking risk, but the more I step into it, the more normal it becomes. Risk is a culture that we create over time. It is a culture created through intentional measures of calculated adventures into the impossible.

RISK IS A NORMAL EXPRESSION IN THE KINGDOM OF GOD

God is the author of risk. He created the earth, allowing evil to reside within His good creation. He created people with a free will, knowing we would have the choice to obey or disobey Him. He took even more risk by putting two trees in the Garden of Eden so that Adam and Eve would have an opportunity to display their loyalty.

God continued to demonstrate risk when He gave humankind responsibility to take care of the Earth though He could have done a much better job of it. He took risk when He chose Israel to be the sole option to prepare the way for the Messiah to rescue us from the curse of sin and death, resulting from the bad choice Adam and Eve made in response to the temptation of satan in the Garden.

God took risk when He allowed His only Son, Jesus, to come into the world to save us from those bad choices we had made to disobey Him. He did this, knowing that satan was going to severely tempt Jesus and that there was a possibility that He would not submit to the disgrace and suffering of the cross. Thankfully, Jesus modeled risk in the Garden of Gethsemane when He finally decided to face the impending suffering on the cross, being separated from His Father for the only time in eternity.

Jesus continually took risk while He was here on Earth. For example, He risked when He reached out and touched the leper when it was religiously illegal to touch someone who was considered unclean in that condition. He took incredible risk when He intervened in the stoning of the prostitute, challenging the religious leaders to throw the first stone, as, I believe, He wrote each one of their sins out in the dirt.

Time after time, we see God taking extraordinary risk throughout human history. He revealed remarkable risk when He made us His representatives of the Kingdom of God here on Earth, especially in light of Adam and Eve's failure when given the same opportunity.

Nonetheless, we are told that, *"we are therefore Christ's ambassadors, as though God were making His appeal through us..."* (2 Cor. 5:20). So, in a sense, God has tied His hands behind His back and put duct tape over His mouth, relying upon us to take responsibility. God took radical risk, knowing that we could misrepresent Him or not do anything at all in being His hands extended to heal and His mouth declaring the good plans and purposes He has for each person.

I often hear people pleading with God to heal their family members or friends when God is saying, "You do it!" We tend to ask God to do what He is asking us to do. Jesus said, *"Heal the sick..."* (Matt. 10:8), which is more accurately translated, "You heal the sick...." Before Jesus ascended to the Father, He told the disciples, *"...They will place their hands on sick people, and they will get well"* (Mark 16:18). Clearly, when God determined to rely upon our commitment to take risk, He set the risk factor bar at a high level in order to accomplish His will on Earth.

Certainly, it is not our power that brings healing, for example, but it is our risk that releases the power of God to heal. Peter declared to the crowd at the Gate Beautiful after the crippled beggar was healed, *"...Why do you stare at us as if by our own power or godliness we had made this man walk"* (Acts 3:12). Interestingly, the power of God was only released when Peter reached out and picked the man up. It was only when Peter took risk that strength was released to the man's feet and ankles, enabling him to walk and jump (see Acts 3:6-9).

Moreover, in empowering us to fulfill our responsibility to represent God and His Kingdom here on the Earth, He gifts us, knowing that we can use the gifts for our own evil desires and selfish motives. He blesses us, even though we may not give Him credit or we may use His blessings for evil purposes. He gives us favor, knowing that we could use it for personal ambition. God is the ultimate risk-taker!

Just as it is God's nature to take risk, so too, He built in us the capacity for risk. Having been born again, it is our Christ-like nature to find opportunities for risk. Risk is to be a normal expression of the believer. In fact, it is this God-given capacity for risk that launches us into the impossible Kingdom purposes that He has prepared for us.

Risk is a Kingdom characteristic, however, that is often underdeveloped and underutilized in the believer's life. While we have been created with the capacity for risk, we must cultivate it as we would any other Kingdom characteristic like love, joy, peace, forgiveness, encouragement, and so forth. The Church is to be the culture in which risk-takers of the Faith are equipped, empowered, and activated in their true supernatural destiny.

RISK IS BEST CULTIVATED IN A CULTURE OF RISK-TAKERS

I love the movie, *A Christmas Story*. I find myself watching it nearly every Christmas season. One of my favorite scenes is when Schwartz and Flick are out on the school grounds debating whether or not putting one's tongue on a frozen metal flagpole would cause the tongue to stick to it.

The dialogue escalates from a "double-dare," to a "double-dog-dare," to the ultimate, "triple-dog-dare." Flick finally succumbs to the pressure, and places his tongue on the frozen flagpole, only to be proven wrong, as the fire department is deployed to dislodge Flick's stuck tongue.

Every time I watch the movie, I admire the risk that Flick took to prove his friends wrong. Even though he lost the "dare," I respect his attempt at defying the odds by putting action to his beliefs. How many of us are willing to take radical risk in order to prove that we can accomplish the miraculous when the world says it is impossible?

Jesus gave Peter a "triple-dog-dare" to defy popular opinion when He challenged him to walk on the water.

> During the fourth watch of the night Jesus went out to them, walking on the lake. When the disciples saw Him walking on the lake, they were terrified. "It's a ghost," they said, and cried out in fear. But Jesus immediately said to them: "Take courage! It is I. Don't be afraid." "Lord, if it's You," Peter replied, "tell me to come to You on the water." "Come," He said. Then Peter got down out of the boat, walked on the water and came toward Jesus. But when he saw the wind, he was afraid and, beginning to sink, cried out, "Lord, save me!" Immediately Jesus reached out His hand and caught him. "You of little faith," He said, "why did you doubt?" (Matthew 14:25-31).

In this circumstance, the disciples could not believe that it was Jesus walking on the water—it was humanly impossible, and therefore, He must be a ghost because people just do not walk on the water! I can imagine them confirming to each other that it is impossible for a human to walk on water, while Jesus challenged them with the truth.

Peter then rises up as the spokesman to counter the challenge. I can almost hear Peter and Jesus debating, like Schwartz and Flick arguing on the playground, whether it was possible to walk on water. Jesus cuts right to the chase and moves right to the "triple-dog-dare" when He challenges Peter to prove Him wrong.

In that environment, surrounded by the peer pressure of the on-looking disciples, Peter has no choice but to step out of the boat if he is going to save face with his friends. I could not even imagine the fear that Peter must have felt taking that first step. Without the triple-dog-dare and the egging on of his friends, he may have jumped back in the boat. Instead, he took risk and accomplished the impossible—the supernatural—and walked on water!

When we create a culture that encourages risk to prove that the impossible is possible, people discover that they can do way more than they ever imagined. When we create a culture of risk, anything is possible through anyone.

In our Firestarters class at Bethel Church, we teach the students that God rewards risk. We celebrate when people in the class step out into risk, whether it is giving a prophetic word to one of the other students at their table, giving a word of knowledge in front of the class, or praying for someone to be healed. We teach them that the only way to step into their supernatural destiny as a Firestarter is by developing a lifestyle of risk.

Each week, we ask the students to share testimonies of how they have taken risk to release the Kingdom throughout the week in their neighborhood, workplace, school, among friends and family, and the community at large. We constantly tell them that they have all of the gifts available to them, but that it is risk that allows the gifts to become evident. It is so exciting to hear testimonies of people who had never believed they were gifted until they stepped out in risk.

One Sunday, one of our students shared that he was at someone's house doing a satellite installation when he noticed someone limping across the living room. He shared that the thought came into his mind that he had the ability to help out with the person's limp because he was a Firestarter. He went on that he "chickened out," doing nothing to release the Kingdom of God toward the person.

He sat down to the smattering of light polite hand claps. Immediately, I stood up and explained that, as a class, we needed to celebrate his adventure into risk! "Think about it," I said, "Prior to this experience, he had never even thought about taking risk. This is an amazing breakthrough, and we need to celebrate his journey into his supernatural destiny."

The next week, he shared that he was at another installation where someone had a physical ailment and he actually stepped out in risk, and asked the person to allow him to pray. He concluded that even though he took risk, he did not see breakthrough. This time, there was more clapping than when he had shared the previous week, but it was not at the level that it would have been if the person had been healed.

Once again, I encouraged the class to treat this testimony as if there had been a breakthrough with cancer being healed. I explained that if we support people who just take risk to the same degree that we applaud the miraculous breakthrough, then we will eventually hear more testimonies of the miraculous because more people will be encouraged to take risk. The class stood to their feet, giving a standing ovation in response to the new level of understanding that they had received.

The next week, the same man excitedly shared that he had met a woman who needed healing at one of his installation sites, and as he took risk and prayed for her, she was completely healed! The class erupted in cheers.

Not only was this Firestarter student activated in taking risk, resulting in breaking through into his supernatural destiny, but the other students were also encouraged to attempt risk as well, as they observed the three-week journey of our supernatural satellite installer.

I have found that it is much easier to inspire people to take risk when they are in an environment that promotes and celebrates risk and not success. When I see the effects of risk-taking in other people's lives, I am more apt to attempt the seeming impossible.

I'll never forget when some friends of mine took me to Angora Lake near Lake Tahoe. We climbed up to a 45-foot overhanging cliff above the lake, and all of my friends jumped off with wild abandonment, hooping and hollering all the way down. Their expression of joy caused me to want to go beyond my comfort level and join them in the higher level of risk they were jumping into.

As I gingerly stepped to the edge of the ledge, however, the lake looked like it was a million miles away. Although I had successfully jumped from a 30-foot tower a few years earlier, I felt like I would die if I jumped this extra 15 feet. Contemplating my fate, I decided that if I backed down from this challenge, I would resort to a penchant for safety for the rest of my life.

Most decisions we make in life often determine the direction of our future decisions and actions. So, standing on the ledge, overlooking the water 45 feet below, and hearing the encouraging cheers of my friends to take the leap, I decided that I was going to make a statement about the way I was going to live the rest of my life. I took a leap of faith. I believe that decision prepared me for, and propelled me into, my supernatural destiny.

GO BIG OR GO LITTLE— BUT JUST GO FOR IT!

All of us have a supernatural destiny, but not everyone steps into his or her supernatural destiny. We are oftentimes waiting for God to equip and empower us, when in fact He is waiting for us to take some kind of risk in order to release what we need to represent and reflect His Kingdom in our lives.

In Romans 12:6, the apostle Paul exhorts that, *"We have different gifts, according to the grace given us. If a man's gift is prophesying, let him use it in proportion to his faith."* In other words, our gift is not going to propel us into risk. Rather, our risk propels us into our gift. We must exercise a certain amount of risk in order to step into the supernatural gifts that empower us into our supernatural destiny.

You are probably familiar with the phrase, "Go big or go home," used especially by those who participate in extreme sports. Certainly, that phrase is indicative of the risk required to compete at the highest levels of competitive extreme sports, but it also tends to minimize the risk it might require for someone just beginning in the risk-taking process.

The writer to the Hebrews says that, *"without faith it is impossible to please God..."* (Heb. 11:6). Notice, there is no minimum amount of risk required. Just take some, any amount, and God is pleased. Jesus said:

I tell you the truth, if you have faith as small as a mustard seed, you can say to this mountain, 'Move from here to there' and it will move. Nothing will be impossible for you (Matthew 17:20).

In each of these instances, the amount is not specified—we either have faith, or we do not. In the Kingdom of God, for stepping into our supernatural destiny, a little bit of risk is as effective as giant leaps of faith.

Living a lifestyle of risk is like getting into a pool. Some choose to jump into the water without even testing the temperature, while others prefer to stick their toe in first to prepare them for what is to come. Some people just take the plunge, while others inch into the water. Either way works. The important consideration is that they are getting into the water.

When it comes to taking risk, God is just as pleased when we go big or inch in. The important consideration is that we are taking some kind of risk to step into our supernatural destiny. Risk is simply leaving our comfort level to go conquer a fear factor or believe for what we would consider impossible for us to accomplish.

Most people do not attempt risk because they think that only a death-defying act qualifies as legitimate risk. Standing up in front of people to share a testimony may be a *ginormous* level of risk for some, while for others it is "easy peasy" and, therefore, would not qualify as risk for them. So then, in a sense, risk is relative. What is risk to one person is not risk to another.

Moreover, what may have been risk yesterday may be my new normal today. Therefore, in a culture of risk, we are continually advancing to new levels, which I will discuss in detail in my next chapter.

FAITH IS FAITH

The fact is that Jesus commended people who simply had faith, not their level of the faith. For example, Jesus announced to blind Bartimaeus, "...'Your faith has healed you.' Immediately he received his sight..." (Mark 10:52). The issue was not the quantity of his faith, but the presence of his faith.

When the sinful woman poured out the perfume on Jesus, and then proceeded to wet His feet with her tears, and then wipe them with her hair, Jesus declared, "Your faith has saved you; go in peace" (Luke 7:50). Likewise, when the woman who had been subject to bleeding for 12 years touched Jesus cloak, He said to her, "Daughter, your faith has healed you. Go in peace and be freed from your suffering" (Mark 5:34). On another occasion, "Some men brought to Him [Jesus] a paralytic, lying on a mat. When Jesus saw their faith, He said to the paralytic, 'Take heart, son; your sins are forgiven'" (Matt. 9:2). In each of these accounts, there is no mention of the amount of faith—they simply had faith.

Then there is the story of the Canaanite woman whose daughter was suffering terribly from demon-possession. In an act of risk, the woman got on her knees, saying, "Help me," and then responded to Jesus' denial for help with the words, "But even the dogs eat the crumbs that fall from their masters' table." Amazingly, it was that seemingly simple act of risk that prompted Jesus to action. "Then He answered, 'Woman, you have great faith! Your request is granted.' And her daughter *was healed from that very hour"* (Matt. 15:21-28). From my perspective, the woman's act did not seem like a "great" act of faith, but for her it was, in light of the potential rejection. In this instance, simple persistence was her "chicken line" to release the supernatural power of God.

When the two blind men approached Jesus asking for healing, we are told that, *"He touched their eyes and said, 'According to your faith will it be done to you'"* (Matt. 9:29). Once again, there is no mention of a minimum level required—it is just faith.

When the centurion replied to Jesus that his servant could be healed with just a word from Jesus, we are told that, *"When Jesus heard this, he was astonished and said to those following him, 'I tell you the truth, I have not found anyone in Israel with such great faith'"* (Matt. 8:10). To some, that might not seem like death-defying risk, but for the centurion it was a statement of confidence for the impossible.

When Paul was ministering in Lystra, he noticed a crippled man who was listening to his message. We are told that, *"...Paul looked directly at him, saw that he had faith to be healed and called out, 'Stand up on your feet!' At that, the man jumped up and began to walk"* (Acts 14:9-10). Certainly, there were other people listening to Paul's message, but for this man, it may be that listening, when he had been crippled from birth, was an act of risk, given the probability that other preachers had made promises of healing of his condition with no results.

The point is that we must express some level of risk to release the supernatural power of God. Therefore, if we are not seeing the miraculous happening in and through our lives, then we must evaluate our risk factor. When Jesus went back to His hometown of Nazareth, we are told that, *"He did not do many miracles there because of their lack of faith"* (Matt. 13:58). Mark adds that, *"He was amazed at their lack of faith..."* (Mark 6:6).

So then, whether we go big or go little, it is important that we do something to demonstrate our faith through risk. In developing a culture of risk, it is important to emphasize and encourage any level of risk-taking. As people get used to taking risk, it then becomes a normal lifestyle, enabling them to go to higher levels in their supernatural destiny.

FREEDOM TO FLOP

In addition to applauding any level of risk, we must also be able to create a safe environment for people to take risk. We teach our students in the Bethel School of Supernatural Ministry that they have to fail at least three times in order to graduate from the first year. This mandate communicates that it is acceptable to fail when we take risk and that we reward risk, not success. Students learn that world-changers are risk-takers.

Furthermore, when students know that they can make mistakes and even fail, they are more apt to take risk. Creating an environment that celebrates the process of taking risk over the outcome propels people into a greater level of confidence to attempt feats that they never would have thought possible.

I will never forget a conference at which I was speaking and had brought a group of students as my ministry team. On one particular night, I asked the students to pick out people from the stage and then give them a prophetic word. I encouraged them to step across their chicken line and take some risk in trying to get specific details of the lives of the people they were going to prophesy to that night.

One of our guys picked out a young man who had been in a wheel-chair for several years. Everyone in the church knew this young man and his family, who were all present at the conference that night. As the student began, he launched into several specific words of knowledge about the young man's life and desires. The young man, as well as his family and many others in the congregation, reacted to each word of knowledge with a confused look.

Once the student had finished, I asked the young man whether those words of knowledge described him. With obvious embarrassment, he said that not one of the words of knowledge applied to him. His family confirmed his statement. A gasp rose from the crowd, as if the worst of all tragedies had just occurred. The pastor sank down in his chair a little, probably wondering why he had invited these "false prophets" to the church.

Without missing a beat, I explained to the congregation that while the words of knowledge were inaccurate, this student had done an amazing job—he had stepped way out of his comfort zone in taking risk. I pointed out that the apostle Paul told us to test every-thing and, therefore, had inherently built into the church a provision for prophetic failure.

I expressed that our goal was to provide a safe culture to take risk and that God is pleased with risk, not success (see Heb. 11:6). I told them about how proud I was with this student for taking such bold risk and how I wished we would all be so willing to be wrong. I further explained that we would never be able to go to the next levels of the supernatural unless we created a safe place to try. I con-cluded by encouraging the congregation that they did not have to be perfect in prophesying either and that we would let them practice in our safe environment.

Amazingly, the crowd erupted in applause. Many were activated in their supernatural destiny that weekend because our student modeled a culture of risk, in which we allow going big and flopping. In creating a culture of risk, we must be committed to encouraging and empowering people to attempt the impossible, not only when they succeed, but also when they fall short. Otherwise, we have a fear-based culture in which people are reluctant to take risk.

MY JOURNEY INTO THE RISK FACTOR

I remember when I first moved up to Redding, California, at the beginning of the summer of 2002 to attend Bethel Church. I was putting in a pool and needed someone to help me dig a trench in order to bury the electrical wiring going to the front of the house. It took several days to dig the trench, and on one of the days, I needed some various items from the local hardware store. I took my digging partner, Chris Overstreet, with me.

I soon found that, not only was Chris an amazing digger, but he was also an amazing risk-taker. While at the hardware store, he approached person after person, asking if they needed healing for anything and sharing the love of God with them. Then he would start prophesying to them about the good plans and purposes God had for them and would share words of knowledge about the ailments in their bodies. Those who had earlier denied having anything wrong admitted that the words of knowledge were accurate. Over the course of 30 minutes, about ten people were ministered to, and a few were healed right there in the store!

Now, I had a lot of experience in street witnessing and had even been on the Vineyard National Evangelistic Board, but I had never seen anyone take risk like Chris had that day—and it seemed so natural for him. Conversely, I felt so intimidated by his boldness because I did not feel like I could ever take that kind of risk. At that time, I had to work myself up to even ask if someone felt any better after I prayed for them to be healed at church.

Over the next several weeks, I continually replayed the encounters that Chris and I had at the hardware store. In my heart, I knew that if he could take that kind of risk, then I could as well. So, I started putting my toe into the realm of reaching out to people by approaching people who had obvious ailments.

If someone were on crutches, I would step across my chicken line and ask to pray for them and then ask if they were feeling any different afterward. Each time, I could feel my heart nearly beating out of my chest as the adrenalin raced through my body. Surprisingly, people started getting healed! Soon, I began to get words of knowledge for people regarding the ailments they were suffering from, and they would often get healed as I took risk to pray for them out in public.

Eventually, I came up with the Treasure Hunt model, which utilizes words of knowledge as clues to find people who I would prophesy to or release healing to. Often, they would then invite Jesus into their lives as a result of the risk I had taken to reveal the practical love of God to them.

This method of supernatural evangelism soon led to my first book, *The Ultimate Treasure Hunt: Supernatural Evangelism through Supernatural Encounters*, which has encouraged Christians all over the world to launch into their supernatural destiny as world-changers.

Amazingly, I now lead Supernatural Lifestyle conferences all around the world equipping, empowering, and activating Christians to step into their supernatural destiny through risk. Watching Chris model risk gave me a vision of my potential in risk-taking. Being able to start small also enabled me to even attempt to start the adventure of taking risk in the supernatural.

In cultivating a culture of risk, then, it is important to start somewhere—to somehow start stepping out. It may be a little or a big expression of risk, but know that God is just waiting for you to step across your chicken line into your supernatural destiny. Moreover, when we surround ourselves with risk-takers, it becomes natural for us to become risk-takers, and before long, we are promoting and propelling the culture to others. I think that is why the writer to the Hebrews encourages us to, *"Remember your leaders, who spoke the word of God to you. Consider the outcome of their way of life and imitate their faith"* (Heb. 13:7).

CHAPTER 4

Chad Dedmon ▷▷ **GIANT KILLERS**

In early 2006, my friends and I attended a conference in a sporting arena in the Los Angeles area. Around noon, we found ourselves slightly discouraged because so far during the meetings there had been no demonstration of the power of God. We had come expecting a mighty move of the Holy Spirit. Many times in the past, we had seen outbreaks of the Holy Spirit, yet we found these meetings to be somewhat uneventful. So we took a vote and decided to go get some food. When we were almost to the car, I suddenly realized, *This is not right! We cannot leave the building without seeing the Kingdom of God manifested!*

I told my friends what I was sensing, and we immediately turned around to go back through the front door of the stadium. Right there, we saw a young lady with a large knee brace walking with crutches into the arena, accompanied by her mother. We approached her and asked if she would like to receive prayer and be healed of her knee condition. She explained to us that she had torn her meniscus playing volleyball and would love some prayer for healing. We laid hands on her knee and invited God's presence. She immediately felt incredible heat and ripped the knee brace off of her leg. On her own initiative, she started bending her knee, putting her full weight on the leg, and walking and then jogging around—all the while praising the Lord! Her mom ended up holding her daughter's crutches and knee brace while we all walked into the sporting arena together.

We were so excited about this breakthrough, that we started getting more words of knowledge for people who were walking around outside the meeting. Surprisingly, I got strange looks from Christians who did not want to receive prayer.

My eye caught a couple of junior high aged kids, and one of them had an arm sling. I asked them, "Wouldn't it be cool if God healed your arm right now?" They said, "No, we don't want any prayer because we are waiting in line for some coffee."

I said, "That's fine," and I casually asked the lady in front of them if she had been in a car accident a few months ago and if she had pain in her lower back from the accident. She then confirmed that she had, and I went on to explain that I could have never known this information about her unless God told me. She was surprised that I knew this information and confirmed that what I said was true. She received prayer, and in a matter of seconds, she was completely healed.

The teenager with the arm in the sling who watched this whole scene transpire exclaimed to me, "Pray for me, too!" After he had watched the healing take place in front of his eyes, I could see a new faith erupt out of his spirit. So I asked his friends next to him to lay their hands on him and pray for Jesus to come. I did this because I wanted them to know that the healing could flow through his friends' hands, and not just through mine. I told them to pray for just a few seconds and then let him check it out. He began to do full rotations with his arm, while realizing that he was completely healed.

Everyone in line behind the teenagers couldn't help but notice that God was healing. People began boldly speaking out their prayer requests and two lines began forming—one for prayer, and one for coffee.

We need to keep in mind that when we approach people to pray for them, like these teenagers, they might be a little standoffish or reserved about receiving prayer. They may have never witnessed the Kingdom of Heaven breaking in and the supernatural displayed. Most people do not realize that we possess the power to carry breakthrough into their everyday needs. When we approach people, they may initially say no to us because they may think it will be just a nice prayer backed with no power. The fact is, though, Jesus rests in and on our lives, which means that as we co-labor with Christ, we are conduits of Heaven. When we reach out to others with the love and power of God, all manner of disease, pain, and affliction will go.

Jesus told us in Matthew 5:16, *"Let your light shine before men that they may see your good deeds and praise your Father in heaven."* The word deeds or works is translated from the Greek word dunamis, which means "the power to perform miraculous signs and wonders."[1] The nature that we have been given through Christ is to shine before people with the light of God and to move in the miraculous. We should never shrink back or feel that we have to hide this light we have been given. Instead, we need to be a city on a hill that cannot be hidden (see Matt. 5:14). As we take risk by releasing the dunamis power of God, we will bring glory to our Father in Heaven.

When I first approached the teenager in the line, he looked at me with much hesitation when I offered to pray for him. He simply did not understand what I was talking about. However, after he saw the Kingdom demonstrated, something jumped inside his heart as he realized what is possible with God.

After the breakout of healing in the coffee line, we heard that there was an impartation service inside the stadium. My best friend and I ran to the front of the line to receive impartation through prayer. As we walked through the line, we received prayer from several pastors and leaders, and then we were guided to walk through a hallway back to our seats. Shortly after walking away from the prayer line, we could feel the anointing of God's presence come upon us.

Joaquin and I immediately felt fire come into our hands. We looked at each other and knew we had to give this fire away. The people coming through the prayer line were experiencing God, but not to the level that we were feeling that God wanted to release. The Spirit of God in us became uncontainable; therefore, we knew we needed to impart this fresh fire to those around us.

Everyone who was praying for people had prayer servant badges on, so I pondered if it would be OK for me to pray for those around me. Whenever I am at church or a conference, it is always my desire to follow the protocol in the meetings. However, my main responsibility is to follow after what the Father is doing, and I felt that He wanted to release His fire! The Holy Spirit was wooing the whole group into a place of encounter that far superseded what was happening.

So, we began to lay our hands on people and release the power of God as they came out of the prayer lines. The atmosphere of

God's presence came in such a tangible measure that people started immediately going into heavenly encounters. People were speaking in tongues, having visions of Jesus, seeing angels, laughing, shaking, and crying on the floor! Some were even screaming out different nations as God was commissioning them.

After about 20 minutes of this, we realized that there was a traffic jam and no one could walk through the hallway because of all the people laid out on the floor! Right then, a few ushers approached us and told us that we needed to stop praying for people and let them go back to their seats. I answered, "Isn't this the point of why we are all here—to encounter God?" The usher replied, "No, people are piling up, and it is getting too crazy. Someone may get injured if you don't stop praying. Also, you don't have a badge, so you need to stop."

Wanting to honor those with authority, Joaquin and I looked at each other and agreed to begin to help the people that were experiencing encounters with God to get up off the floor and clear the hallway. In the process of taking risk, we must always remember to honor and respect people. This, however, was quite an incredible experience in which we took risk and got to see God set people free all around us.

One of my core values is to give away what I have and to realize that the Holy Spirit rests on me for the benefit of others. He lives inside of me to guide, comfort, and lead me into all truth. He rests upon my life to release breakthrough for others.

In the Old Testament, God would rest upon the generals of the faith to do great exploits. For example, Elijah ran faster than chariots, Sampson killed many men with the jawbone of a donkey, and Daniel believed God to close the mouths of the lions. In each case, after the incredible exploit was accomplished, the Spirit of God would lift off of God's anointed one.

Jesus introduced a new covenant in which the Holy Spirit rests on all Christians and never leaves. When Jesus was commissioned into ministry and was baptized in the River Jordan, the Holy Spirit came upon Him and remained. Jesus modeled to every believer what it looked like to carry God's presence and impart it to those around Him. We need to understand that the nature of Christ lives in us, in which risk is the key component.

One of the examples of how God has taken risk was with the nation of Israel—by choosing them as His own and calling them to Himself. He led the whole nation out of slavery, through the dessert, and into the Promised Land. God's heart was looking for a people who would take risk so they could co-labor with Him. To show that He was with them in their risk adventure, He revealed Himself to Israel through many miraculous signs and wonders. Some of these included the fire by night, cloud by day, fresh manna, freedom from sickness, and clothes that did not wear out for 40 years (see Deut. 8:4; Exod. 16).

These miracles were supposed to cause the people of Israel to have faith in order to step into and possess the enemy's territory, believing that God would protect them and give them the victory. God was backing up His promises to Israel, but He did not force them to go into the Promised Land. He always loves to give us a choice and partner with our desire to accomplish His purposes. Israel needed to respond by saying yes to God's promises and activating those promises by taking action. However, unbelief crept into their hearts, and the people of Israel lost their faith, their connection with God, and their desire to be led by Him.

In Numbers 14:11, God asks Moses, "...How long will they refuse to believe in Me, in spite of all the miraculous signs I have performed among them?" In this Scripture, I personally believe God is not angry, but sad. He was disappointed because He had invested His heart into this nation. The people of Israel had not chosen to respond to His investment by softening their hearts and displaying through action their faith. Instead, the nation of Israel began to complain, grumble, and actually believe it would be better for them if they were back in captivity in Egypt. They could have chosen to be ignited in their hearts by the miracles that God performed among them, moving into a place of action to possess the Promised Land.

This snapshot of Israel reveals their calloused hearts and unbelief that eventually turned into disillusionment and deception. The end result was a backslidden state.

On their journey to the Promised Land, they were always advancing forward toward their inheritance. They decided to stop and camp at the edge of the Promised Land and make an evaluation of whether or not to continue on the journey. After getting a negative report back from ten and a positive report back from two of the spies, they had to decide which report to believe (see Num. 13).

As they began to be consumed with the negative report, they actually believed (and were deceived to think) that God was leading them to their demise. This was their opportunity, however, to have the eyes of their hearts opened to see that God was bringing them into their victory.

God never sets us up for failure, but always positions us for success. He is so great that He will even use the plan of the enemy and work it out for our good (see Rom. 8:28).

Fear paralyzes us from moving forward, but faith enables and activates us to step into our destiny. We can never let fear dictate our frame of mind and decisions. Just like the Israelites, we must continually look forward into the promises of God. When we look backward, we come to the same conclusion that life is more comfortable as slaves to the enemy. As the people of God, we are called to never look backward or to backslide.

Moreover, backsliding can also look like staying stagnant in our hearts, like a body of water that is not moving; we are called to always be moving forward. Stagnant water is polluted and becomes a breeding ground for disease, but moving water always brings life. Bill Johnson often says, "We are called to be a river, not a lake."

God became so frustrated with Israel's backsliding and unbelief that, in Numbers 14:12-17, God told Moses that He was ready to destroy Israel because of their unbelief and rebellion. Moses intervened by telling God that that was not a good idea because the Egyptians and the surrounding nations knew about the promises that He had made to Israel.

Amazingly, God took further risk by not destroying them, but partnering with Israel and taking them into the Promised Land. To do so, however, He had to raise up a new generation. God decided to keep His promise and not destroy Israel. He raised up a new generation—Joshua's generation, people who were full of faith and willing to take risk in partnering with God. God is looking to raise up a generation of giant-killers, a generation that transcends gender, race, and age. God can use anyone.

One of my favorite quotes by a powerful prayer warrior and father in the faith, Lou Engle, states, "A giant's destiny is to fall!" A giant's destiny is to be killed by the Lord's anointed, and it is imperative that we do not just stand by and let giants mock the armies of the living God.

Some people in the Church try to ignore the enemy and think he will just go away. Not so! We are not supposed to focus on the enemy, but we do need to acknowledge that there are giants who live in the Promised Land of our destiny, and then we need to take them out.

As spiritual warriors, it is imperative to have the same spirit and response that David had. When a whole nation was paralyzed with fear, David basically said to the king, "If no one will kill this giant, I will because I know the Lord is with me."

When we see giants, we cannot look at them and let fear rule our hearts. We have to confront the fear in our hearts before we can face the enemy. Even if we have fear, we must submit that fear to the Lord and focus on His victorious character and goodness in the midst of the battle.

There are many giants that can live in our land, such as poverty, disease, divorce, and disunity. God is releasing a generation who takes a stand and confronts the enemy and says, "Not on my watch!"

I was a junior high pastor for several years, and the young people I worked with were giant-killers. They all prophesied, moved in signs and wonders, and healed the sick. It was commonplace for my wife and me to arrive at church on a Sunday morning for the youth service and to have those precious ones get down on their knees and literally beg us to take them out into the community to do evangelism. They were fearless when it came to stepping out in the supernatural and "doing the stuff." We tried to create a culture in which it was normal to reach out to others while going about their everyday lives. As a youth pastor, I would pinch myself as I listened every week to new testimonies of people getting healed and saved.

One week, a testimony was shared about two 12-year-old girls who went swimming at the local community pool for the day. They were busy playing in the pool, laughing, and racing to the diving board, seeing who could make the biggest cannonballs. Suddenly, one of the girls felt the Holy Spirit come on her, and she began shouting out, "Does anyone here want to know Jesus?" The daughter of a nearby Muslim family, who was 11 years old, responded, "Yes! That's me!" They prayed with her right there to receive Jesus.

They were so excited and full of faith after what happened that they decided to leave the swimming pool and go to a nearby mall to find people to pray for. They got a word of knowledge about someone having neck pain from a car accident. They found the lady with the neck pain and asked her if they could pray for her. They prayed, and she was completely healed.

One of the benefits of being a youth pastor is that a new batch of kids comes in every year that you can mold and shape into revivalists. One Sunday morning during one of our services, we all divided up into groups and went out into the community. In my group, I had three new sixth grade girls, and we were going out into the community to do a treasure hunt.

In doing evangelism over the years, I have found that adults can be wary of another adult approaching them and asking to pray for them. However, the great thing about having junior high aged kids with me when doing a treasure hunt is that I experience the exact opposite; many adults who are hard-hearted or difficult to reach will often respond with openness and welcome a prayer from kids.

So, with these kids, we would all get words of knowledge, and then I would encourage them to approach the "treasure" (person we find on our treasure hunt who fits our description). We would then ask if we could pray for the person highlighted on our treasure map.

This particular time, we were in the parking lot of McDonald's, and I saw an older couple off in the distance. I suddenly got a word of knowledge for back pain and directed the three girls to approach the couple and ask if they had any back pain. With big smiles, they skipped over to the couple to ask them the question.

When I got there, the lady was nodding her head indicating that she had back pain. I asked, "Would it be all right for the girls and me to pray for you?" She agreed, and we all took turns praying for her. One of the girls said, "Jesus, I pray that this monster in her back would leave! When Jesus comes, monsters can't stay, so Jesus comes into her back." Meanwhile, I was praying that the little girl saying there was a monster in her back didn't offend the lady!

After we prayed for her, I asked her how she was feeling. She responded, "When the little girl prayed for the monster in my back to leave, it felt like a lightning bolt hit my spine, and all the pain left!" She then explained how 10 years ago, in the Senior Olympics on the basketball team, she broke her tailbone and her lower lumbar disc had slipped. A few years later, she was in a car accident, which further increased the back pain, and therefore, she had needed to get her spine fused. Since the fusion, she had suffered from incredible pain and limited mobility.

She started dancing, laughing, and doing back bends, and there was no pain! We ended our time with them by dancing in the parking lot celebrating this miracle together. The young girl who prayed for this woman had a pure and willing heart to step into her destiny. I have learned that God always breathes on pure hearts and the willingness to take risk.

I'll never forget another Sunday morning when I was in the parking lot conversing with some friends between services, and a band of junior highers came from out of nowhere—screaming, laughing, and carrying crutches with them. They came over to me, and I asked them what had happened. They told me they saw a woman walking in the parking lot of the church with crutches and an ankle brace. They ran over to ask if they could pray for her, and she agreed. They prayed for her, and her ankle was instantly healed. They were full of joy and excitement after seeing this miracle, knowing that this kind of breakthrough was what they were called to walk in. They were so excited that they wanted to share it with everyone they saw that day.

These junior highers taught me how to live in childlike faith and wonder. Jesus told His disciples that they couldn't enter into the Kingdom of Heaven unless they became like a little child. In Matthew 18:3-4, Jesus tells us,

"...I tell you the truth, unless you change and become like little children, you will never enter the Kingdom of Heaven. Therefore, whoever humbles himself like this child is the greatest in the Kingdom of Heaven."

My constant prayer is that I will continue to cultivate a childlike heart for the rest of my life. It is my desire that even well into my old age I will be known as someone who had the faith of a child.

One of the sobering aspects of youth ministry is that whatever you preach, they believe. A youth pastor helps to shape the beginning stages of a young mind's perspective on who Jesus is and what it looks like to be a Christian. When I told my youth group that everyone is called to heal the sick, they believed me, and they began to see healing manifest in their own lives.

Another positive aspect of youth ministry is that young people have not developed a filter for disappointment. Helping people to move past their own failures, broken dreams, and promises and to begin to dream with God again is one of my main goals of ministry. In Proverbs 13:12, Solomon tells us that *"Hope deferred makes the heart sick, but a dream fulfilled is a tree of life."* By creating a culture of dreaming with God, we invited our kids to co-labor with Jesus and take risk, all while developing their spiritual gifts in a safe place.

I would consistently take these teenagers with me to regional events (as a part of my ministry team) when I was invited to come and speak in the Southern California area. At one of those meetings, I called out this word of knowledge, "There's somebody here with deafness and someone else with a leg shorter than the other." Right then, an older lady stood in response to the word for deafness. I released my junior high kids to minister. They prayed for the lady with deafness in her ear and then whispered something next to her ear to test out her hearing. To her surprise, she could hear their whispers!

The junior high students also prayed for the other lady who needed her leg to grow out. Immediately, her shorter leg grew out to the normal length. She stood up to check out her leg and discovered that she was totally healed with no more back pain. As soon as this miracle happened, many different people who needed healing in their bodies started coming to the front, and the teenagers began to pray over them. I took a moment and smiled to myself as I observed my kids stepping into their destiny. I continued to hear more amazing reports about people getting healed and touched by God.

The heartbeat of Jesus' ministry was to model to humankind how to be a son or daughter in right relationship with God. He shaped and molded 12 men who became His disciples. One might think He would have chosen CEOs, senators, or proven leaders in society to represent Him. Yet He chose common, unproven men. He gave the keys to the Kingdom and trusted His life's ministry to these disciples when He left the Earth. I want us to look a little more specifically at Peter and Judas. These two disciples were very similar—they had amazing potential, yet had moments of failure in their lives.

Peter was a fisherman, and because of his outgoing personality, he usually spoke or took action first before any of the other disciples—he was a risk-taker. Jesus took an incredible risk when He told Peter that he would be the rock upon which He would build His church. In Matthew 16:18, Jesus declared, *"And I tell you that you are Peter, and upon this rock I will build My church and the gates of Hades will not overcome it."* Jesus had eyes to see Peter's potential and calling before anyone (even Peter) could see it. When Jesus declared this word over Peter, it was in response to Peter's recognition of who Jesus was.

Interestingly, I believe Peter was highlighted because of the risk he took. When Jesus asked His disciples the question in Matthew 16:13-16, *"Who do people say the son of man is?"* the disciples replied that people said He could be Elijah, Jeremiah, or one of the other prophets. Jesus then turned the tables on the disciples and asked them, *"Who do you say that I am?"* Peter was the one who took risk. He was the only one who responded with revelation from Heaven, *"You are the Christ, the Son of the living God!"* Like Peter, we must take risk to enter into our supernatural destiny.

When Jesus was walking on the water and invited all of the disciples to come and walk with Him, Peter was the only one who readily responded to His invitation. It took a lot of risk and courage to be the only one to get out of the boat during a storm. Peter was a forerunner for the Body of Christ. He may not have done everything correctly, but he had passion and zeal.

Some people who are forerunners can be a little rough around the edges and might say or do things in certain instances that can be perceived as too zealous. We need to always remember that the condition of our hearts before the Lord is more important than others' perceptions of us. If we have a lot of zeal for the Lord, our hearts are in the right place, and we are teachable, then we will end up maturing and living in God's best for our lives.

You never find Jesus apologizing for the mistakes of His disciples. This is because Jesus' leadership style also embodied risk. He taught His disciples to be powerful and to have great influence, living as an extension of His heart to the people. Jesus was not the kind of leader who withdrew responsibility or position from His disciples, even when they disappointed His heart. He always gave them opportunities to be powerful.

For example, Jesus saw that Judas had an anointing to steward finances, so He put him in charge of the money. The very thing that Judas was anointed for destroyed his life in the end because of the bad choices he made. Judas gave the keys of his gifting over to the enemy when he let greed rule his heart. Jesus gave Judas an opportunity to overcome temptation by giving him this opportunity. However, Jesus never did override Judas' freewill.

This is the same way that Jesus operates with us. He calls us into our gifting and trusts us, allowing us the chance to steward what He has given us. Sometimes people's weaknesses can become their greatest strength when they are given the freedom to work it out. As leaders, it is necessary to model Jesus' leadership style by creating a safe place where people can grow in their gifting. Judas was one who allowed failure and bad choices to mark his life. Judas will be forever remembered for his compromise. However, Peter repented, moving past his failure and denial of Jesus, and he walked in courage, resolve, and faith for the rest of his life.

When taking on the junior high pastor role, I was initially hesitant because I had the wrong mindset of what junior high ministry was. I saw this role as a glorified babysitting position. At first, I thought I would be putting kids in a padded room, entertaining them with movies and pizza parties, and hoping all the kids would survive the night without killing each other or me. God actually rebuked me and said, "Chad, you are called to raise up revivalists, whether I put you in the nursery or the convalescent home." So, that's what I set out to do.

After I began this journey, I realized that it was my greatest honor and privilege to be a junior high pastor because I got to watch lives constantly get changed and transformed by God. They, in turn, changed their world within their families and friend's lives and at their schools. They forever touched my own heart with their passion and love for God through their willingness to take risk.

I learned a powerful principle throughout that time—when Jesus lives inside of us, we have destiny and are giant-killers, no matter our age, gender, or social status. It is essential for us to always allow Jesus to mold and shape our hearts, lives, and attitudes so we live lives of risk in order to step into our destiny.

ENDNOTE

1. James Strong, Biblesoft's New Exhaustive Strong's Numbers and Concordance with Expanded Greek-Hebrew Dictionary (Seattle, WA: Biblesoft, Inc., 1994, 2003,2006) G1410.

SECTION 3

DEVELOPING SUPERNATURAL LEVELS OF RISK

CHAPTER 5

Kevin Dedmon ▶ **KAIZEN RISK**

When I got my first driver's license on my 16th birthday, I was 5 feet 6 inches tall and weighed 105 pounds. Actually, I lied to the Department of Motor Vehicles, telling them that I weighed a whopping 110 pounds because of my embarrassment about being so underdeveloped. I was a junior in high school, and was shorter and skinnier than most of the freshman class, including the girls. Consequently, I was continually mistaken for a freshman during my first three years of high school, and at the beginning of each year, I was inevitably initiated by some upper classman that had not noticed me on campus the previous years!

Now, I have always loved sports. Before high school, I was an all-star pitcher in Little League, a star running back in Pee Wee football, a primary scorer in AYSO soccer, and a blue ribbon winner in the 50-yard dash at the Washington State Junior Olympics. Unfortunately, I stopped growing at the age of 12 for some reason. Subsequently, as I entered into my high school days, I found that I was no longer picked for any of the teams that I tried out for because of my size and lack of strength.

In my freshman year, I was relegated to the tennis and golf teams, which in those days were considered to be wimp sports. I "lettered" in tennis, but was ashamed to wear my "letterman's" jacket because everyone would laugh and tease me because of the tennis racquet attached to the "letter," indicating the sport I represented. Only a few parents ever came to watch our matches, and we only had six players, which was the minimum required for a match against another school.

I *liked* tennis, but I *loved* football, baseball, and especially basketball. I would practice shooting basketballs for hours with the hope that I would one day miraculously grow and be able to play on my high school team. I became a prolific shooter, but never even thought about trying out for the team because of my small stature.

So, shortly after my 16th birthday, I decided I was going to do something to accelerate my physical development. I had been noticing ads in various magazines highlighting men who had overcome the same physical deficiencies that I was plagued with. You have probably seen these ads—the ones with the guys who are magically transformed overnight from pencil-necked wimps to muscle-bound hulks.

I was sold. I bought an entire case of the protein powder concoction that promised to transform me into the big man on campus. After reading the instructions, I quadrupled the amount suggested. I figured that the added doses would propel me into the muscle-bound vision that I had for myself.

Along with the protein powder, I decided I needed to work out. I had a friend, who had previously tried to convince me to lift weights with him, but I had made excuses, covering up my embarrassment at barely being able to lift the 45-pound bar, let alone any weight added to it! Going to a weightlifting gym was out of the question, but lifting weights with a friend who would certainly expose my ineptitude was way more intimidating. But now I was desperate.

So, after weighing myself, I drank a quadruple dose of protein powder and went to my weightlifting friend's house, telling him that I was ready to be transformed. I confessed my fear of embarrassment and made him swear to secrecy.

I worked out for about two hours, exercising every muscle group from head to toe. I did several sets of curls, squats, bench presses, lunges, pulls—you name it, I did it. Afterward, I felt throbbing pain in muscles that I never knew I had!

I remember going home feeling so confident that my entire life was going to be transformed because of the new regimen I had initiated. I went to bed that night exuberant over the change that I would surely see in the mirror and on the scale the next morning.

When I woke up the next morning, I could not move. I had so over-worked the tendons and ligaments throughout my body that, as I slept through the night, I had somehow curled up into a fetal position as each of those tendons and ligaments contracted. My legs were positioned as though I had jumped from the high-dive, preparing for a cannonball. To make matters worse, I could not straighten my arms—they were locked against my chest as though I was preparing myself to be baptized.

As I rolled onto my back with legs stuck in the cannonball position and arms clutching my chest, every muscle group that I had exercised cried out in searing pain. My entire body was a cumulative throb.

It took about 30 minutes to stretch out my arms and legs so that I could get out of bed. As I inched my way to the mirror, excitement began to escalate within me as I anticipated my new huge hulk image. What I found, however, was very disappointing. To my chagrin, I actually looked smaller than I did the day before!

Even worse, when I got on the scale, I saw that I had lost two pounds! I was horrified. *How could I have lost two pounds when I took all of that weight gain protein powder that promised that I would be transformed into a muscle-bound hulk?* I was left feeling hopeless—my plan had failed. I never weightlifted again, and I threw the rest of the gross-tasting protein powder in the trash.

Interestingly, the summer after that horrible experience, I became a Christian going into my senior year. I also grew 6 inches over the next ten months and gained about 50 pounds by the time I graduated. All I did was consistently eat. There was one occasion during the growth spurt when the manager of an all-you-can-eat buffet restaurant cut me off! I pretty much ate, played basketball and tennis, and slept a lot during those months of my senior year.

I'll never forget the day the basketball coach approached me in the gym after noticing me playing basketball with some friends. Thinking I was a freshman, he asked if I was planning on trying out for the team the following year. He assured me that I would have a spot on the varsity team, even as a sophomore because of my excellent jump shot and the potential of filling out my now six-foot frame.

He could hardly believe it when I informed him that I was graduating the next week, and that I had been in his P.E. class my freshman through junior years. Needless to say, he was very disappointed that he had not found the next generation star for his basketball team. If only that protein powder had transformed me when I really needed it the year before!

A few years later, after growing another inch and weighing about 180 pounds, I did get to play basketball for L.I.F.E. Bible College before transferring to Vanguard University to finish my B.A. degree in Biblical Studies. I still play basketball, but these days, I'm working on a transformation program to reverse my growth—in width! This transformation process is much more difficult and seems as futile. I am still waiting for the miracle!

GOING TO NEW LEVELS

In reality, transformation does not normally happen in a day. We cannot expect to grow physically, emotionally, or spiritually without a consistent, continual commitment toward change.

In Romans 12:1, the apostle Paul commands us to be transformed, which, he instructs, takes place by the renewing of our minds. Likewise, in Ephesians 4:23-24, Paul encourages us to "... *put on the new self,* [which is] *being created to be like God in true righteousness.*" In the Greek, Paul uses the present tense in both of these verses for the verbs, *renewing* and *being created*, which implies a continual sense.

In other words, we are to put ourselves into a position in which we are continually renewed, leading to transformation. Thus, transformation is a process, not a one-time, all-inclusive event.

Thankfully, this change toward new levels of growth is not completely dependent upon our own efforts. We have been given the Holy Spirit, who helps us in this process. In Ephesians 3:16, the apostle Paul prays that *"...He* [God] *may strengthen you with power through His Spirit in your inner being...."*

Interestingly, in Ephesians 4:23-24, Paul uses the passive voice for the verb *to be renewed,* which indicates something that is done to us. He then uses the active voice for the verb *to put on,* indicating something we do. So then, in this process of transformation, we find ourselves in a partnership; we are to continually activate—*put on*—the *renewal* God is giving us.

These principles apply to growing in faith as well. God gives us the grace to go to the next levels, but we must take the risk that releases us into the next levels of faith. I would like to wake up one morning and possess the levels of faith that I so admire in other people who take incredible risk to release the supernatural realm, but I know that I am going to have to partner with the grace that God has extended to me, inviting me into my personal supernatural destiny.

Risk, then, is similar to weight training (yuck!) in the sense that, once we have conquered a certain level, it becomes a natural routine—a normal expectation. In order to be risk-takers, living by faith, we must continue to grow and stretch ourselves in greater measures. We must continue to go beyond our comfort level if we expect to accomplish the seemingly impossible.

As we commit ourselves to developing our Risk Factor, we must be willing to push on things that seem unattainable for our current risk level. We must be committed to pushing the envelope of our current breakthrough to step into our destiny.

The apostle Paul exhorted Timothy to continue to push the envelope in every area of his life, including risk, when he said, *"But you, man of God, flee from all this, and pursue righteousness, godliness, faith, love, endurance and gentleness"* (1 Tim. 6:11). In other words, we must *pursue* faith as a continual lifestyle. More importantly, risk will not chase us down—we must pursue it, looking for ongoing opportunities to seize the moment.

I got my first pair of skis on Christmas day when I was 10 years old. I was so excited. Immediately, I went outside with my new boots and skis to work on my balance as I stood in the snow on our front yard. In my mind I pictured myself flying down a mountain.

My first adventure on the ski slope, however, was not flying down a double black diamond expert run. Rather, I spent several days on the bunny hill. I found that there was a big difference between standing in my front yard imagining myself flying down the mountain, and actually doing it! Once I conquered the bunny hill, I was ready for the rope tow, then the T-bar, then the chair lift, and then on to the bigger hills.

I'll never forget the first time I attempted a black diamond expert run. I looked down the steep slope and cautiously began traversing back and forth, scared out of my mind. It was not long, however, until I simply aimed my skis down the mountain and took off with complete confidence as I accelerated to the brink of insanity in perfect stylistic form. Eventually, I got to the point where I could even ski "out of bounds" and jump off of and over giant boulders.

How did I get to the point where I could ski so effortlessly while taking such extreme risk? I simply took gradual, increasing levels of risk, resulting in growing confidence as I conquered each new level of risk.

I love the story of David coming to the battlefield where Israel was waging war against the Philistines, and finding Israel's army paralyzed by fear (see 1 Sam. 17). The giant, Goliath, had been challenging someone from Israel to take risk to fight him. The Israelites' response, astonishingly, was to hide in the safety of the rocks, ignoring Goliath's insults, which were designed to elicit a response of risk, to cross the chicken line into battle. The Israelites obviously had little or no confidence in God's ability to help them defeat the obstacle represented in the giant before them, leaving them derailed from their destiny for victory.

David, on the other hand, had confidence in God's desire and ability to help him defeat the giant. Remarkably, David was not even a warrior, although he had experienced God's assistance previously when he had killed the lion and the bear. Importantly, those victories gave him confidence in his present opportunity to take bigger steps of risk.

David used his previous testimonies of successful risk as fuel for his faith for the next level, enabling him to accomplish the seemingly impossible in killing Goliath. More importantly, that next level of risk propelled him into his destiny to be the king of Israel and become the anchor of the lineage of the Messiah, Jesus.

Often, the key to killing the Goliaths in our lives is to start with a lion or a bear. Once again, increasing in faith is like weight training. If you have maxed out at 200 pounds on the bench press and decide that you want to reach 250 pounds, you have to eventually try to lift the weight. You may not be able to lift that heavier weight, but as you make the attempt, you are preparing yourself to be able to lift 225 pounds.

GOING TO NEW EXTREME NEXT LEVELS

Once people have experienced a certain level of risk, over time that level becomes their normal, requiring them to go for more if they aspire to be risk-takers. Risk-takers continually go for the more, the bigger, the extreme, and the impossible.

I love watching the X Games because the athletes are continually pushing the envelope of the impossible. In each event, the competitors are trying to accomplish death-defying feats that were previously unthinkable—like doing a double back flip on a motorcycle while flying more than 50 feet off of a ramp or executing a Double McTwist 1260 on a snowboard while being launched 15 feet above the 18-foot high wall of the super-pipe.

Risk-takers believe that anything is possible, and they are willing to prove it by sacrificing their bodies to continual injury in their attempts to prove it! In reality, if we do not attempt to do something new, out of the box, or dangerous, risking some kind of failure and loss, then we will never create anything new. Nearly every invention or innovation has come about as a result of someone taking risk to try something new and seemingly impossible. We might even say that *the incredible* is not possible unless it seems impossible.

T.S. Eliot once said, *"You have to risk going too far to discover just how far you can really go."*[1]

There have been a few times when I have gone too far in taking risk, leading to adverse consequences, but more times than not, I have regrettably stopped too soon because of fear, only to realize later that I missed out on an amazing opportunity for adventure or blessing. In order to go to the extreme next levels of risk, we must be willing to fall short of our goal. When we go for too much, however, we will often find that we end up accomplishing more than if we had never tried for the impossible.

I was in Haiti a few weeks after an earthquake devastated the capital city of Port of Prince in January 2010. One of the days we were ministering in a small suburban community looking for people who needed medical help. We had several nurses and doctors on our team, as well as those who were solely equipped with faith to believe for supernatural intervention to heal the sick, injured, and diseased and to raise the dead.

We came to the center of a particular community where the U.N. troops had just dropped off rice, beans, and water. An angry crowd had formed next to one of the dilapidated buildings. At first we thought a fight was breaking out over the distribution of the food and water, but we soon learned that the commotion was over a woman who had just collapsed and died on the side of the dirt road.

It was obvious that the crowd had seen enough death. They were expressing their anger over this woman, who had appeared to survive the earthquake, but because of undetected internal injuries incurred during the quake, had finally collapsed and died. It felt like the crowd was at a tipping point of disappointment; they seemed to be on the brink of rioting, as the yelling and fist pumping permeated the atmosphere.

Something came over me as I approached the mob. I turned to my team and exclaimed, "Let's go raise her from the dead!" They nodded back their support of the bold risk I was about to take, given the volatile crowd surrounding the dead woman. Before fear had an opportunity to dissuade my seeming stupidity, I began yelling, "Medical, medical...." Amazingly, the crowd parted as our medical doctor held up his stethoscope as a sign that we were there to help. Everyone was silent as our doctor confirmed what the crowd already knew—the woman was indeed dead.

I could sense the rising raging reaction to the news, as it was passed throughout the crowd. At that moment, I decided that I needed to change the atmosphere before the crowd turned on us in violence. Throwing all caution to the wind, I yelled out, "Who wants to see this woman raised from the dead?" They all erupted with approving cheers.

I could see in their eyes that they were desperate for something good to happen, so I began to prophesy that it was time for life in Haiti and that God was going to reveal His goodness to them. Once again, the crowd responded in ecstatic unison, as they began to shout, "Vive, vive, vive (live)."

The team and I began to declare life into the woman as the crowd looked on with hopeful anticipation. We were so full of faith, but after about 30 more minutes, I could sense that the crowd was becoming restless and losing hope. So, I decided to change the atmosphere again. I began to call out words of knowledge for ailments represented in particular people in the crowd.

Healings started breaking out throughout the crowd as each word of knowledge was acknowledged. Over the next 45 minutes, the team and I continued calling out words of knowledge, and many more were healed. Among the many who were healed was a woman healed of blindness. Another woman had a cancerous tumor dissolve.

I'll never forget the guy who came up to the crowd riding a bicycle. After observing our revival outbreak for a few minutes, he began yelling, "F*** you," over and over, accentuated by extending one finger of his right hand. Over his obvious disdain of our presence, I shouted out a word of knowledge for someone with a torn rotator cuff. Immediately, the man's right hand retracted, covering his left shoulder. He looked at me in dismay—his left rotator cuff had been completely healed!

We did not see the breakthrough we were expecting for the woman who had died, but as we attempted to lift 250 pounds, so to speak, we were able to see amazing miracles because we took risk to go to the next extreme level in trying to raise someone from the dead. We must be willing to go to new levels of risk if we plan on fulfilling our supernatural destiny.

The apostle Paul certainly was concerned for the risk factor of the Thessalonians when he wrote, *"Night and day we pray most earnestly that we may see you again and supply what is lacking in your faith"* (1 Thess. 3:10). He then celebrated their risk level in the next letter he wrote to them, reflected in the following compliment, *"We ought always to thank God for you, brothers, and rightly so, because your faith is growing more and more..."* (2 Thess. 1:3). Faith was never meant to remain static, but to be a dynamic growing lifestyle.

Elsewhere, the apostle Paul encouraged the Corinthians in the following exhortation, *"Excel in everything—in faith, in speech, in knowledge, in complete earnestness and in your love for us..."* (2 Cor. 8:7). In other words, every area of our lives should be geared toward growth—including our lifestyle of risk.

CREATIVE LEVELS OF RISK

The Japanese have a term, *kaizen,* which means "continual improvement." W. Edwards Deming, a quality control expert, originally developed the philosophy of *Kaizen.* Having been rejected by U.S. corporations, he offered his new concepts to Japanese business leaders shortly after World War II. The Japanese implemented his *Fourteen Points of Management* into many of their businesses and soon became the leaders in innovation and efficiency. Now they have become one of the most prosperous nations in the world.

For the Japanese, *Kaizen* has come to incorporate every area of life. They have become a culture that wants to go to the next levels—to continually improve. As a leader, Paul was a proponent of *Kaizen*, evidenced by the following prayer: *"...Our hope is that, as your faith continues to grow, our area of activity among you will greatly expand"* (2 Cor. 10:15).

Risk is a key characteristic required to go to the next levels of creativity, strategic thinking for inventions, innovations, as well as accomplishing miraculous feats. I believe it is time for the Church to be the leaders in these areas. Moreover, I believe God is releasing a grace on the Christians these days to be the forerunners of risk.

My wife, Theresa, who oversees all of the prophetic arts in our School of Supernatural Ministry at Bethel Church in Redding, California, is an amazing activator in teaching people to take risk in creativity. She teaches that everyone has some level of creativity, but that many have been stifled because someone told them, or implied, that they did not measure up to the undefined creative standard. As a result, they stopped taking risk and then stopped growing.

Theresa constantly encourages her students to go to the next levels of extreme risk in releasing the arts in reaching out to people in order to communicate God's heart and purposes for them. She equips, empowers, and activates people to go way beyond what they previously thought possible in their own abilities, as well as in the supernatural being released through their artistic expressions.

As a result, we have seen many people healed as they have simply held a painting. We have seen many healed through a picture of a stick figure with a red X locating the part of the body needing healing. Amazingly, God uses any act of creative risk to release His Kingdom into people's lives.

One day, one of her students, Francesco, who happens to be an accomplished artist, decided to take a new level of risk in releasing the supernatural. He simply took a piece of chalk with him to the downtown Redding area looking for divine appointments. Seeing a man limping toward him, Francesco stooped down to the sidewalk and drew a simple square with the chalk.

As the man came upon the square on the sidewalk, Francesco asked why he was limping. The man explained that he had torn the ligaments in his knee and was in tremendous pain. Francesco, full of faith, promised that if the man would just step into the center of the square, God would heal him because there was a portal of God's presence in the square.

Skeptically, the man stepped into the center of the square. Francesco stepped back, watching, as the presence of God instantly healed the man's knee! Francesco was then able to witness to the man about how Jesus had just touched his knee.

So, when did the portal of God's presence show up? Did Francesco see the portal and then draw a square around it? No, Francesco believed that if he drew the square on the sidewalk, God would come and fill it with His presence—and He did! That is the nature of risk: God fills the squares of our efforts of risk with His presence and releases His supernatural power.

Jesus said,

I tell you the truth, if you have faith and do not doubt, not only can you do what was done to the fig tree, but also you can say to this mountain, "Go, throw yourself into the sea," and it will be done (Matthew 21:21).

So then, the mountainous levels of risk we are willing to speak to will determine the level of breakthrough we will experience.

Your mountain may be taking a piece of chalk and drawing a square on a sidewalk or trying to raise a woman from the dead in front of a hostile crowd. Whatever your chicken line is, believe that crossing it will lead you to the next level of breakthrough as a world-changer.

I want to have the same attitude as the disciples when they pleaded, *"Increase our faith"* (Luke 17:5). I continually ask God for the grace and then the confidence to take greater levels of risk to realize my enormous supernatural destiny.

SUPERSIZE YOUR FAITH

People will sometimes ask me to pray for them to have a double portion of the miracles that I have seen. My prayer, to their chagrin, is that they will have the grace to take double the risk that I have taken. Usually, their eyes get wide with fear because they know that I am committed to taking crazy amounts of risk in releasing the Kingdom of God in supernatural healing. They were hoping for the supernatural ability without ever considering the risk factor!

The fact is that we can know all of the Kingdom keys to unlocking healing, but they do us no good unless we step out of our comfort levels, cross the chicken line, and take risk. We can get impartations from others who have broken through in greater measures of healing, but at some point, we must activate what we have received by taking risk to release what has been deposited.

Jesus said, *"Give and it will be given back to you in the measure you have given, pressed down, shaken together, and running over..."*

(Luke 6:38). Similarly, in the parable of the minas, those who took risk to invest what they had freely received were rewarded with more (see Luke 19:11-27).

We can experience amazing levels of intimacy in His presence, attend amazing conferences, read incredible books, hear anointed Bible studies, and receive impartation after impartation, but at some point, we have to step out and take risk in order to activate what we have received. Then, amazingly, we will get the "more" that we are so desperate for.

Certainly, there is "more" available than we are experiencing today. I need more breakthroughs in order to step into the destiny Jesus declared when He said, *"I tell you the truth, anyone who has faith in Me will do what I have been doing. He will do even greater things than these, because I am going to the Father"* (John 14:12).

My interns are radical risk-takers, constantly daring each other to take extreme levels of risk. We have created a culture in which pushing the envelope is normal. This past year, my interns came up with a new game that they call, "Risk Dare."

The game is played as each person in the group gets an opportunity to dare someone in the group to take some kind of crazy risk to release the supernatural. This is accompanied by doing some kind of crazy, embarrassing performance, like singing, rapping, dancing, painting a picture for someone on the spot, or making up a poem that would also communicate God's heart for them.

The "Darer" then will select a person or a crowd of people that the "Risker" will address. Once the "Dare" is completed, the "Risker" gets to choose a "Dare" for one of the other interns. My interns are very creative at upping the ante each time!

The benefit has been that each of the interns has been stretched beyond their comfort level in ways that they never thought of before. Fear and intimidation have been broken off of them, and it has become easier for them to take risk in any situation. Moreover, they are now prophecy and healing machines as a result of the growth that has occurred through the game they have played.

So then, may you receive the grace and the confidence needed to get into the "game." Even more, may you continue to grow in new levels of extreme creative risk as you pursue your dreams and destiny in fulfilling God's plans and purposes in you and through you.

ENDNOTE

1   T.S. Eliot, Preface to *Transit of Venus: Poems* by Harry Crosby (1931).

CHAPTER 6

Chad Dedmon ⟫ **ACCEPTING THE INVITATION INTO RISK**

When I was 18 years old, I read a book compilation called *Jesus Freaks*, which is about Christians around the world who have given their lives for Jesus, accompanied with various kinds of persecution. The book also included stories about people who had supernatural encounters when God provided for, protected, and saved them during times of great desperation and need. These people would have encounters with angels or would see Jesus manifest in the natural.

After reading this book, I began to hunger for these same supernatural encounters to happen to me. I reflected upon the numerous accounts of passionate people who were unafraid to share their love for Jesus and who gave up everything for the sake of the Gospel.

I evaluated how these people were constantly encountering a supernatural God and how, in my life in California, I was not experiencing God in the same way. I started studying in the Bible where Peter and Paul would see cities turned upside down through signs and wonders. My heart began crying out to see this same dimension of God manifesting in my life.

Somehow, it was no longer OK for me just to read about the God of Daniel, David, Peter, and Paul. Instead, this same God had to become a tangible reality in my life. Hebrews 13:8 states, *"Jesus Christ is the same yesterday, today, and forever."* If I truly believed this Scripture, I knew I needed a change in my heart in order to see God revealed in my own life. I finally came to the conclusion that I should go and visit one of the countries that the book talked about where these radical supernatural encounters were happening.

Shortly after finishing the book, I had an experience with the Lord in the middle of the night. He spoke to me audibly and said, "Pack your bags; I am sending you to the nations!" That same phrase echoed through my mind for two days solid, and I knew God was calling me out. I didn't know which country He was calling me to.

So I began to press into God for direction and guidance. A few weeks later, I received an invitation from a friend to go to Africa. I immediately thought, "This must be God opening up a door for me to go to the nations." so I started saving my money to prepare for the journey ahead.

Shortly after this, I attended a concert by Delirious, one of my all-time favorite bands. While I was in the middle of the concert and singing along to my favorite worship song ever, "Obsession," with my eyes closed and hands raised up, I felt someone put his hand on my chest and begin to speak in tongues. Whoever it was started prophesying over me saying, "You are called to the nations; the islands are waiting for you." I opened my eyes to see that it was Martin Smith, the lead singer of Delirious. This was another confirmation for me of God's leading, and I felt energized about what was going to happen for me in the nations.

So I decided to put Africa on hold and pursue going to the islands (which is good news for me because I also love to surf). After a little research, I found out that most of the persecution of Christians going on at that time was in Indonesia. In addition, Indonesia was also where some of the most radical supernatural encounters were taking place. I suddenly knew in my spirit that this was the place God was calling me to go.

I talked to my parents about the idea of going to Indonesia to preach the Gospel, and they asked, "What do you know about Indonesia?" I answered, "Well, I know it is a place where many different supernatural experiences are happening and also that it's a good surf spot!" They said, "OK, let's pull up on the Internet some news about it and see some of the current events going on." We looked at Indonesia's main newspaper, *The Jakarta Post*, and discovered the cover story, "Hundreds of Christians killed by Moslems." Without skipping a beat, I looked at my parents and said, "Yep! That's where I am going!" My parents looked at me uneasily and encouraged me to find a missions organization to connect with so that I could be a part of a team.

I started to pray for direction and researched some different missions organizations. All the while, I felt God speaking to my heart that I wasn't supposed to go with a team or organization. So I told my parents the great news (or so I thought), and they strongly stressed that what I heard could not be God. They began to give me words of wisdom about why it would be important to go with a team and told me to go back into prayer, suggesting that I should also fast.

As I went back to fast and pray, I heard the audible voice of God telling me, "I will go with you, and I will be your covering." After hearing this word, I felt total peace and confidence that God was going to protect and guide me as I entered into this crazy adventure. After I shared what I had heard with my parents, they felt the same way.

Just before leaving, I had a friend who decided he wanted to go to Indonesia as well, which was great because that meant I didn't have to travel alone. When we arrived in the country, a friend picked us up from the airport and brought us to the beach. While on the beach, I saw a man walking and heard the Lord speak to me in a detailed way about his life. So I approached him and explained to him what I felt the Lord was saying for him: that he was a spiritual father in Indonesia and was going to raise up many pastors and leaders. He told me that he had started schools of ministry all over Indonesia and that the majority of the schools were for pastors. He was so touched by the word I gave him and began to open up the doors for me to go and speak at these schools.

God is so good to provide exactly what we need when we step out in faith after He speaks to us. This began my wonderful and fascinating exploration of Indonesia. I went to 20 islands in four months and preached in many schools of ministry and churches through this divine appointment connection I made on the beach.

During this time, I was enrolled in the school of the Holy Spirit and learned a lot about the nature and heart of God. At this point in my life, I had no official training in ministry or in the gifts of the Spirit. I was just a 20-year-old following God and saying yes to who He is and what I read in the Bible about what He can do. I was eager and full of zeal to travel as much as possible in order to take advantage of my time there, and I journeyed by moped, boat, bus, and plane.

On one occasion, my interpreter and I had to hike all day in the jungle to reach a village of 150 people who had never seen a white person before. My interpreter asked me to do a healing service for the church. At that time, I did not have a full understanding of our role as believers in the area of healing ministry.

My idea of healing ministry was that God was sovereign and mysteriously came to heal whenever He felt like it. I did not understand that we could co-labor with Jesus in the healing ministry, bringing Heaven down to Earth. In First Corinthians 3:9, Paul writes, *"For we are God's fellow workers; you are God's field, God's building."* That night, I preached on healing and prayed a corporate prayer for people who were sick or in pain to receive a touch from God, but to my shock, no one was healed. I was very disappointed, discouraged, and dissatisfied by that result. Interestingly enough, the village pastor thanked me and asked me to do another healing meeting the next night.

In the morning, I was struggling with the feeling of failure and everything inside of me was saying, "You will have the same results as last night." I made the decision to move beyond my disappointment and take another risk by inviting God to come and heal the people in this village.

As I started to pray and prepare, the Lord gave me an open vision of the church service that night. In the vision, I was washing people's feet, and as I did so, people were getting healed. I was getting stirred and excited as I connected with God and what He wanted to do in the service rather than being consumed with the thoughts of last night's disappointment. Similar to people in Bible times, the villagers walked around in sandals, so their feet get extremely dirty, and a foot washing is very much appreciated. In the vision, I was using my best outfit as the rag to wash everyone's feet.

That night at the meeting, I did end up using my best (and my only clean) outfit to wash everyone's feet, just as I had seen in the vision. As I began doing this, the Spirit of God broke into the meeting, and people began to weep as they discovered that all the pain and sickness was leaving their bodies. A lady with debilitating arthritis was brought in by her friends on a grass mat to the meeting. After I washed her feet, she started running around completely healed. Another lady, who had had cataracts for a number of years, started screaming, "I am healed!"

In the midst of all these healings, one stood out to me—a little boy who was born deaf and mute. I washed first his feet and then his whole family's feet. The boy's ears opened, and he started to make noises with his tongue and formed his first word. We all rejoiced and worshipped God for this miraculous display of love and power.

I am so happy that I moved past disappointment and took risk again, remembering that God always wants to show up—even if we are hesitant for a moment or don't know what we are doing. He will guide and lead us into what He wants to do.

There are moments in our lives when we take great risk that will release breakthrough and cultivate an open Heaven. Going to Indonesia was one of those moments for me. We are called to be on a constant journey with the Holy Spirit on which each step forward is with the footsteps of faith. Sometimes we face present circumstances or "people's wisdom" that would try to tell us not to take radical steps of faith. We need to discern when He is asking us to get out of the boat (our comfort zone) and step out into the unknown, where we will see the miraculous begin to manifest.

Up until that point in history, no one thought it would be possible to walk on water. When Peter stepped out of the boat and into the unknown, the law of gravity didn't affect Him; He supernaturally defied gravity. In that moment, Peter's faith turned into action; he was not focused on the thoughts or concerns of the other disciples. He didn't inquire of their wisdom or advice about the invitation that Jesus had given. He responded wholeheartedly and without hesitation, while keeping his eyes on Jesus (see Matt. 14:23-31).

Faith requires action. James 2:26 says, *"For just as the body without the spirit is dead, so also faith without works is dead."* Faith should be the life source and motivation for our deeds. Faith is tangible. We cannot let ourselves be surrounded by people who are living in doubt or unbelief, but a community of those who believe they serve a God with whom anything is possible.

We all have dreams in our hearts and prophetic words we have been given that have not come to pass yet. There are times when God invites us to take risk, and when we follow His leading, He opens up the doorway for our dreams and prophetic destinies to be fulfilled. It is to our benefit that we recognize when God is breathing on our dreams.

One of these invitations from Heaven happened to my wife and me in the spring of 2008. At this time, Julia and I were serving as youth pastors at a local church in Southern California, and we loved what we were doing. We were equipping the youth and drawing so much life from the community we were building.

One of the positive aspects of living in a prophetic culture is that we receive words about our destiny, but we don't always know when or how God will bring them to pass. I had received several prophetic words from prophets, spiritual mothers and fathers, and friends about going to the nations and preaching the Gospel. My spirit was in agreement with these words, but I was in a place of tension while I waited to see how they would come to pass. I would frequently take short-term mission trips and see outbreaks of God's Spirit, but I would always come back home wanting more.

God does not only speak to us through prophets and prophecies, but in many other ways. Kris Vallotton explains it this way, "God's first language is not English." God speaks to us through the language of His Spirit, and it is our job to tune in and listen to what He is saying.

One way that God speaks to me is through movies. A few years back, I kept on hearing about a movie called *Blood Diamond* and wanted to see it. As I walked into the evening showing, I saw that I was the only one there, which is very unusual for a Southern California movie theater. As I began to watch the movie, I realized that God had cleared out the theatre to create the environment for my heart to be undone for the nations. Throughout the movie, I wept and interceded for the injustices I saw. I felt bad for the people who were going to sit in the movie seat after me because I had dripped snot all over the chair.

Another way God speaks to me is through paintings. During this time, I was working at a church, and we would meet weekly in the prayer room for our staff meeting. The youth had recently redecorated the prayer room with prophetic art paintings. One of the paintings read, "He is calling you to the nations. Do you hear His voice?" Every week, this painting would catch my eye during the meeting, and I realized that a part of my heart was longing to come alive to touch the nations of the world.

God was starting to spark something inside my heart because He knew I was ready to accept this invitation to step into my dreams. God never gives us dreams to tease us, but to invite us into a deeper relationship with Him. In April 2008, I was spending time with one of my spiritual mothers, Heidi Baker. That night, we were at a conference that Bill Johnson was speaking at, and he ended the night by inviting everyone to join hands and pray for the nations. I thought to myself, *This should be fun. I will be praying with Heidi Baker, who is a mother to the nations.*

As soon as we started praying, I fell out under the power of God and was immediately taken up to Heaven where I saw the Father. He told me that it was time for me to step into the next season of my calling, and He was commissioning me to be a father to the nations. I suddenly heard Heidi Baker praying over me, "Chad, I see the Father speaking over you, and He is saying, 'I am releasing you into the next season of your calling; you will be a father to the nations!'" Heidi began to pray and intercede for this next season in my life.

The next day my wife Julia and I began to pray about this encounter that I had and what we were called to do in this season. She had had a similar experience several years earlier in which God told her, "Mother the nations," in an open vision that lasted for several hours. She had been preparing her heart since that time for an opportunity to go and begin to fulfill this assignment. A couple days later, we attended a Benny Hinn meeting. When Pastor Benny saw us, he proclaimed, "Thank God you guys are here. Can I meet with you after the service?"

After the meeting, Pastor Benny explained to us that he had been having dreams about us going to the nations and felt that we were presently in a season of God commissioning us to go. He asked us, "Have you ever gone to Israel?" We responded, "No, but we love Israel and have such a heart to go and visit." He then invited us to go to Israel and be a part of his tour with all of our expenses paid. Julia and I looked at each other in shock and said that we would be honored and privileged to go to Israel.

That same week, someone felt that we were being commissioned to the nations and decided to invest in us by writing us a personal check and in the memo they wrote—"for the nations." We began to process these supernatural events and realized that God was releasing momentum and confirming His word to us.

Not only was God breathing on our dreams, but He was also providing for our dreams to become a reality. After all of these events took place to confirm God's leading in this direction, we could not just deposit the check "for the nations" into our personal checking account and continue living our lives as normal. This was an invitation for us to receive a radical shift and move forward into this direction for our lives. We knew that God was calling us to begin to be a father and mother in the nations of the world.

As a result of all these events, my wife and I decided to transition out of being on staff at the church where we were working, leave the comforts of living in a home, put everything in storage, and buy two around-the-world tickets for our new adventure. Some of our friends were concerned about whether we were making the right decision by leaving the stability of a paycheck. There were moments of apprehension for us because of the economic recession that had just hit America, and we started to see the strength of the U.S. dollar decline.

We also had a very difficult time saying good-bye to the youth we had been pouring our lives into for the previous three years. They were so dear to our hearts, and we knew that saying good-bye would break our hearts.

We asked ourselves, "Is this really a wise decision to go and travel with no stable income or specific plan in mind?" As we prayed about it, Julia and I had a total peace and faith that began to arise in our spirits. We knew that we had a green light ahead of us as we stepped into this direction that God was calling us to. When we booked our tickets, we picked the destinations where we would be landing for each leg of the journey. We settled on choosing to go to the countries we had always had a heart for and a desire to visit. In most of the countries on our itinerary, we didn't know anyone, but we knew God was calling us to go, and He would connect us as we went.

This adventure ended up lasting for over a year, traveling full-time and living out of our suitcases. We were constantly amazed at how God orchestrated divine relationships with different friends and leaders. We had spiritual fathers and mothers who introduced us to churches along the way, and most of the time we would get in touch with our new connections just a few weeks before we went to the next destination.

God far superseded our expectations with His goodness and kindness on the trip. We were able to visit and enjoy over 14 nations and meet many new friends on every continent of the world (except Antarctica). We were able to cross socio-economic lines and see the world in a way that is rare to the average traveler. We were able to take in a wonderful aspect of the cultures we visited because we seldom stayed in hotels, but with the local people, to further enrich our experience in the culture. Down to the last detail, we were provided for and taken care of by God.

When we were in Israel at the beginning of our one-year journey, we had the opportunity to visit for about a month. We were able to partner with Joaquin Evans to help host a healing conference in the heart of Jerusalem. During the conference, we had the chance to equip the youth of Israel in power-evangelism and take them out into the community.

When my team went out, we decided to go through the Old City. We walked up to one of the city gates and discovered a crippled man sitting down. I interviewed him to find out what he needed prayer for. He explained that he had four large tumors on his upper leg.

We began to pray for him and asked if there was any difference in his pain levels. He told me that if he would move his leg in a certain way, excruciating pain would follow. So I asked him if he would go ahead and try to move his leg around. He took a leap of faith and moved it. Just as he did, his jaw dropped open and he started shouting in Hebrew, "There is no pain!" He patted his leg to check if the tumors had shrunk and realized that they were completely gone. He jumped up to his feet and began to dance around. He started showing us all of his books and magazines about rock climbing that he had been collecting.

He told us that for the last three years, while he had been suffering with these debilitating tumors, he couldn't walk or do much of anything physical, and therefore, he was unable to pursue his dream of rock climbing. He started crying and thanking us for helping him step into his dreams. What a wonderful day in the Kingdom to see a crippled man healed and his dreams restored at the city gate.

Before I went to Israel, I had been in Costa Rica on a surfing trip and lost my wedding ring in the water. Julia and I agreed that we would get another wedding ring when we got back from Israel. One morning, I heard the Lord tell me, "Chad, why don't you get a ring that represents your covenant to your wife in the land of covenant?" I thought this was a good idea, so I went in search of a ring.

Before going into the jewelry shop, I was praying and getting words of knowledge for the healing service that I would be facilitating later that night. I had written down some names and conditions in my notebook. I took the notebook with me into the jewelry shop because I was going straight over to the service afterward.

As I was looking at rings, I noticed that the clerk's name was Thomas. I had written down the name "Thomas" and then "metal in the left ankle" underneath his name in my notebook. I asked him if he had metal and pain in his left ankle. He said yes, and I showed him the page in my journal where I had written it all down.

I then asked if he believed that Jehovah could heal him. He said yes, and so I prayed for him, and without laying hands on him, I started speaking and declaring, "God is going to heal your ankle right now!" Right away, God's tangible, electric, wonderful presence filled the atmosphere of the jewelry store.

I asked the clerk if he felt anything going on in his ankle. He said, "I feel extreme heat and the sensation of lightning bolts going up and down my left leg." I asked him to do something that he couldn't do before. He told me that he couldn't stand tiptoed because of the metal in his ankle. He tried to stand tiptoed and realized that he could do it. The sales clerk was in shock that God had just healed him. I then asked him if he could continue helping me find a wedding ring. The customer service was really good after that point because he was so happy he was healed.

My wife and I had many wonderful adventures on this trip. One of the incredible memories we had was when we were in Pemba,

Mozambique, at the children's center (called the Village of Joy) at Iris Ministries. We were fortunate enough to be there during their Christmas celebration, which included songs, gifts, and lots of food—Africa style. We tagged along with Heidi Baker and her team throughout the day and helped pass out gifts to toddlers, children, and teenagers in the Village of Joy.

We watched in awe as one of the little toddlers was given a chocolate bar in his gift bag and by the look on his face, we knew he had never tasted or received anything like that. As soon as he tasted a bite, he became conscious of how good it was, and immediately wanted to share his chocolate with all the other little babies around him. He started passing out his whole chocolate bar piece by piece to his friends and was so happy to give it all away.

We got to experience the joy on the children's faces as they received their new toys. It moved our hearts to watch these children, who were initially raised in poverty, be rescued, loved on, taken in, and embraced by spiritual mothers and fathers from Iris Ministries as they received the heavenly Father's love. They were now moving in radical generosity and sharing their gifts with one another—what an incredible transformation.

From the world's perspective, they had very little possessions, but from the Kingdom's perspective, they were living in abundance and had it all. Julia and I sat there stunned and found ourselves with tears in our eyes as we watched these children living in a feast of thanksgiving as they received these Christmas gifts.

We love going to Africa to pour ourselves out and serve the needs of Iris Ministries, but the main reason we go is somewhat selfish. Every time we are there, our hearts become softer, and our lives become more transformed and changed into the image of Jesus as we experience God in the midst of the Kingdom culture that has been established there.

I would encourage everyone to go and be involved in Iris Ministries. Your life and heart will never be the same. It is a special place where a community of believers is walking in the spirit of adoption and love, radical faith, and miracles on a daily basis.

Another one of our favorite places is New Zealand. We had always known that God had called us individually and together to this nation. As we were speaking and ministering at one of our favorite churches, I gave a word of knowledge that God wanted to heal runners and those who had a desire to run who had injuries that kept them from running. Instantly, the healing presence of God began moving and healing people with running related injuries. One man came forward and told me he woke up that morning and heard the thought in his head, *Wouldn't it be great if I ran today?*

I interviewed him and asked him about his injury. Several years earlier, he had fallen through a glass roof and died; the paramedics brought him back to life. The doctors did surgery and had to physically remove his Achilles' tendon and calf muscle. He was left with limited feeling below the knee and restricted mobility and feeling in his lower leg and foot.

We prayed for him and watched as God touched his leg. After a little while, He was able to put his heel all the way down to the ground for the first time since the accident. I pressed my fingers down onto his feet and asked, "Can you feel this?" He did a double take and said, "Yes, I could feel your hand touching my foot." I asked if there was another way that he could test it out to see what God was doing. He said, "Well, I can't run."

So I looked at him full of faith and said, "You are going to run tonight, and I am going to run with you!" Immediately, we began to sprint together from one end of the stage to the other. He was smiling ear to ear and gave me a big bear hug after we ran together. That was when he realized that he was healed because he had not been able to run since the injury. His wife, as well as the rest of the congregation, was looking on and praising God for this beautiful miracle.

One of the most stunning cities we visited on our trip was Capetown, South Africa. We had many adventures there and also saw several wonderful healings. One of my favorites was when I was ministering and praying for healing at a meeting in a township just outside of the city. A mother brought her 3-year-old boy up to the front and explained that her son had not yet been able to walk. She had taken him to the doctor, yet they had no explanation for why he couldn't walk. Her son was asleep in her arms, and she requested prayer for him. I took his legs and declared over him, "You will run!" I was gently moving his legs as I declared this word over him.

When releasing healing, it is always good to have the person in need of healing check out the condition so that they can take notice when God is beginning to touch and heal their bodies. In John 5:8, Jesus spoke to the crippled beggar and told him to take up his mat and walk. Some people feel timid to check out their ailments after prayer to see if anything has shifted in their pain level, but this lady was quite the exception.

I began to explain to her (through an interpreter) that she should check out her son's legs to see if there was any difference after he woke up. However, she thought that I meant that she should check it out right at that moment. To my shock, she violently shook her son awake. The moment his eyes halfway opened, she dropped him feet first. To all of our surprise, he landed on his feet and began running down the aisle. Everyone started screaming and praising the Lord. What an amazing miracle of healing we saw that night.

We also got to enjoy the beautiful island of Fiji and were extremely excited to find out that one of our friends had set up our full itinerary and organized accommodation for us. She wanted to bless us so that we would experience the authentic Fijian culture, as well as have the opportunity to minister to the people there.

We received our itinerary for the month and found out that she had connected us with one of her friends who owned a private island resort where we would be staying for a few days. After traveling through many foreign countries and staying in all kinds of accommodations, we were ecstatic about the thought of relaxing at the beach on a private island resort.

As we landed, exited the boat, and beheld the beauty of the island, I turned to my wife and said, "Honey, we are in the FOG" (My good friend, Chris Overstreet, coined the phrase "FOG" to mean "favor of God."). When you take risks and partner with Heaven, it will release another dimension of favor upon your life.

Favor is given to you, not only for your own blessing, but also for the breakthrough of those around you. While we were on the island, we were presented with the opportunity to minister to the resort staff members. We gave a short message, prophesied, and released healing, and they were very thankful. This made our blissful time on the island complete because we got to see the Kingdom of God come and bless others around us.

God is inviting us all on an amazing adventure with Him. He is asking us to go where He is and move side-by-side with Him into unknown and uncharted territory. There are innumerable exploits waiting to be apprehended by believers who will dare to execute the courage to take huge risks in the Kingdom.

Bill Johnson says that when we get saved, "we receive a draft notice in the Spirit that we have been commissioned to advance the Kingdom of Heaven." I believe we, as a generation, are entering into a season of invitation from Heaven like never before. First John 3:8 says, *"The son of man was made manifest to destroy the works of the devil."* We are called to have the same lifestyle as Jesus. There are many ways to display the Kingdom, but love and the miracle-working power of Jesus will always destroy the works of the devil.

When we operate in our identity in Christ, we will be able to abide in an open Heaven. The Father will gaze upon us as His dear children with absolute pleasure. Now is the time to accept His invitation to go deeper in our relationship with Him and step out into the unknown through risk.

SECTION 4

BREAKING THROUGH
THE FEAR BARRIER

CHAPTER 7

Chad Dedmon >> **TRY, TRY, AND TRY AGAIN**

In 2002, I attended the Bethel School of Supernatural Ministry. Kris Vallotton, the director of our school, told us that, in order to graduate, we had to take risk in the supernatural and fail at least three times. He explained that, by doing this, we would begin to grow in the supernatural and in our intimacy with Jesus as we stepped out and began to exercise our faith.

We would frequently practice hearing from the Lord and the prophetic so that we would increase in accuracy whenever we had the opportunity. What we learned inside the four walls of our school, we took outside of the classroom and practiced what we were taught. A word of encouragement could be something simple that connects the listener to the heart of their heavenly Father. For example, you could encourage with a word like, "Your smile brings life to those around you" or "You have a healing anointing coming upon your life in a greater measure." When the prophetic is coupled with the word of knowledge gift, the level of risk in the delivery of the word can sometimes dramatically increase.

My classmates and I would often go out to eat, and we made it a point to each get a prophetic word for our server. After we ate, we asked the Father what He was saying about our server. On one occasion, I kept on hearing the phrase, "I like my little brown house." I also began to hear the name "Vicki," so I glanced at the server's name tag to check if it said Vicki. It didn't, so I asked God for clarification and was not hearing any response.

Meanwhile, my friends started to give her words of encouragement. Honestly, at this point, I just wanted to have a simple word to give her from God. I was scared that if I gave her what I had gotten, she would think that I was a spiritual "fruit loop" and leave with a bad taste in her mouth about the prophetic and God.

My moment of truth came when it was my turn to prophesy. So, I went for it and asked her, "Does the name Vicki mean anything to you?" As I was saying this, my legs were shaking under the table because I was so nervous. She took a step back and said, "Wow, that is my middle name!"

Encouraged by her response, I gave the second word I had gotten. I explained to her that I kept hearing the phrase, "I like my little brown house." Immediately, she put her tray down on the table, and in an intense tone of voice asked if I had been talking to her husband. I replied, "No, I don't know your husband." She explained that she and her husband had been having a discussion that very morning about selling their house. She had been saying the phrase to him, "I like my little brown house." She asked me how I could possibly have known about that conversation. I told her I didn't know, but God did, and He cared about every area of her life.

So, I asked her if she had any pain in her body at the moment. She told me she actually did have pain in her lower back from a car accident she had been in ten years earlier. We all prayed for her back, and the pain left. I learned from this situation that not only does God want to speak into people's lives about personal things going on, but He also cares about healing physical pain.

At times, we can receive information from God about others that goes beyond our understanding; it will not make any sense to us. However, the person receiving the word will often understand its meaning. When we receive a prophetic word or word of knowledge for someone, it is important to not be introspective about whether or not it makes sense to us. It usually won't make sense to us because it doesn't apply to us.

Later that night, I contemplated what had happened at the restaurant and remembered how extremely nervous I was before I delivered the word to the server. It was intriguing to me that I had received accurate information from God about her life, but was so scared to tell it to her. I carefully thought about why I was so scared to do the very thing I am called to do—encourage people with the word of God. Have you ever taken a step back from your life to evaluate your fears?

I then asked myself another question, "When I see people in a wheelchair in public and have a desire to pray for them, why does fear consume me?" Why would I be scared of the following scenario: I approach a person in the wheelchair, ask if they want to be healed, and pray for God's healing presence to touch them. At this point, they may get completely healed, jump out of the wheelchair, and begin to praise Jesus while everyone around is watching the miraculous, raw power of God released. The ripple effect of this miracle will influence friends and family and they will see the miracle-working power and love of Jesus become tangible in their life! I thought, *What can possibly be scary about that?*

According to Second Corinthians 10:5, we need to learn how to take every thought captive under the obedience of Christ, because the spirit of unbelief can speak in the form of our personal thoughts. For example, the thought could sound something like this, *What if this doesn't work, or what if this person doesn't get healed when I pray?* These thoughts arise from the fear that we will fail if we try and also from the fear of people.

At some point, we will have to choose to conquer our fears and not let fear dictate our decisions. However, when fear is overcome, that doesn't necessarily guarantee that we'll never have to deal with fear again. Fear can continue to show up at our doorstep, but the choice is up to us whether or not we will open the door and welcome it in.

Every time we resist the inclination to submit to fear, that choice builds our spiritual muscles to be able to resist fear and embrace faith. Interestingly, there are still plenty of times that I will feel apprehensive before praying for someone in the marketplace. When I feel fear, I know that the enemy is present and is trying to keep me from stepping into my destiny in that moment.

I always try to move in the opposite spirit of what I know the enemy is trying to do in any given situation. I remember as a boy growing up in the church, people would tell me, "When the enemy reveals himself in a situation, it is usually because it is the last card that he can play." With that in mind, I am able to use fear for my advantage like a thermometer to gage what God is about ready to do. Whenever the enemy tries to shout at me with the accusations of intimidation and fear, I take courage because I know my destiny in God is getting ready to be revealed.

Throughout the Bible, we see many examples of the heroes of the faith who struggled with fear before they stepped into their breakthrough. When Moses died, God chose to promote Joshua as the leader for His people Israel. God commissioned Joshua to take the people across the Jordan River and into the Promised Land. There was a tangible fear that awaited them when they stepped into the Promised Land because of the giants that lived in the land. In Joshua 1:5-7, God told Joshua:

No man will be able to stand before you all the days of your life; as I was with Moses, so I will be with you. I will not leave you nor forsake you. Be strong and of good courage, for to this people you shall divide as an inheritance the land in which I swore to their fathers to give them. Only be strong and very courageous, that you may observe to do according to all the Law, which Moses my servant commanded you; do not turn from it to the right hand or to the left, that you may prosper wherever you go.

When Joshua had this encounter with God, he was told twice to be strong and courageous. Here, God gave Joshua one of the secrets of living in breakthrough and prosperity; it is to be strong and courageous and live a focused life. It is our responsibility to live in faith and to focus on what God has commanded us to do; we cannot live in fear and be consumed with what the enemy is doing.

The generation that died in the desert could not move past focusing on the size of the giants that lived in the Promised Land (or from another perspective, the impossibilities that awaited them). God's original intention for His people was to get them to leave captivity, pass through the desert, and dwell in the Promised Land. Because of the fear that paralyzed their hearts and the unbelief that blinded them, they were unable to partner with God's purposes and plans for their lives.

Consequently, they were sent back into the wilderness, which was only meant to be a transitional location that brought them out from slavery and into a place of promise and freedom. However, because the children of Israel made bad decisions, they could not move forward, but spent the rest of their lives in a transitional place, where they died. Do you want to move forward into the Promised Land of destiny or stay in a place of transition?

Having the right focus and heart intentions will cause us to see the Promised Land that is right in front of us. When we allow fear to paralyze us, we are unable to advance into our destiny. By focusing on what God is doing, we can advance the Kingdom of God. Additionally, in the area of healing, it is important to always focus on what God is doing. When praying for people, it is sometimes easy to become discouraged when we find out after we have wholeheartedly prayed for someone that nothing really happened or it is only a little better.

In any given situation, I am constantly looking for where and how God is moving. If I get a response like, it is only maybe a little better," I get more specific and ask questions like, "What do you mean? Is the pain leaving? If zero means 'none of the pain is gone,' and ten means 'all the pain is gone,' where do you think you are at?" If the response is "one," then I get really excited and start praising Jesus.

I go on to explain, "Jesus is touching you, and if we hadn't prayed, you would still be at a level zero! You are in the middle of

God touching your body." I encourage them not to focus on the lack or be discouraged because they are not yet completely healed, but to celebrate the breakthrough. As we focus on what God is doing and begin to move into thanksgiving, we will see increase.

We are not supposed to overcome fear all alone; we need to surround ourselves with friends and spiritual fathers and mothers that will come alongside and help us to conquer our fears. My best friend is my wife Julia. The first movie we went to when we were dating was *Bruce Almighty*. Throughout our dating and married life, we've loved going to the movies. However, we didn't go to the movies until about four months into our dating experience.

I was especially excited to go on our first date to the movies because of the romantic ambience that can happen. We were 21 years old at the time, and I don't know about you, but the reason why I paid over $20 for the movies, extra popcorn, and Milk Duds is because of the chance to put my arm around the girl of my dreams and wait for her to whisper sweet nothings into my ear.

Toward the end of the movie, my wish was coming true. Julia leaned over to whisper into my ear. I thought, *Here come the sweet nothings.* I heard her say softly, "The Lord just told me to give an altar call in the movie theater." She looked at me like I was supposed to do something. I thought, *Wow, that is the best sweet nothing I have ever received. I knew that this girl was something special.* I said, "You got the word! Go for it! I am here to be your ministry team and to catch them when they fall." That's all the encouragement she needed.

We immediately got up and started walking down toward the front of the movie theater. Julia began preaching the Gospel and sharing about the Father's love. Bruce Almighty is the perfect movie to use to preach the Gospel because it is all about how we each have a special invitation to touch the Father's heart.

This all happened just as the movie was ending, so she was warring with the sound of the ending credits. Some people were trying to listen and some people were just leaving. Suddenly, Julia ran out of the movie theater and left me there. I later found out that she felt the fire of God and felt that she needed to start running. I picked up where she left off, wrapped up her message, and invited people to pray with me to receive Jesus. I think people felt sorry for me, so they bowed their heads to pray.

I walked outside the theater and found her in the parking lot in front of the movie theater talking with two guys with an intense expression on her face. As I walked up to them, I could hear her starting to prophesy over them. She started getting words of knowledge about their lives and told them, "I see you in your room. You have a black comforter on your bed. Beside your bed is a red desk, and on top of your desk, you have Geography, History, Math, and English books. Over your bed you have a map of the world. You have pinpointed India, Russia, and Asia, and you are attending university right now to learn how to teach English. God wants to give you the desires of your heart and allow you to travel and teach."

Toward the end of the word, one of the young men started poking my shoulder and curiously asked us, "Are you aliens?" We laughed out loud and began to explain how there was no way that we could have known these details about their lives, but the God of the universe knows these things about them, and He desires that they would know Him personally. I asked, "Do you want to be best friends with the Creator of the universe?" They both said yes, and we led them in a prayer to receive Jesus into their hearts. We also invited the Holy Spirit to come and fill them.

Right there, in the parking lot of the movie theater, they fell down and started shaking under the power of God. Someone driving by stopped when they saw the two guys shaking on the ground and asked, "Should we call 9-1-1? Are they having a seizure?" We explained, "No, they are OK. They just received prayer, and God is touching them. Do you want us to pray for you, too?" They said, "No way," rolled up their window, and quickly sped off. Afterward, we introduced the guys to our friends, who attended a local church in the area, so they could get connected with a body of believers.

From Heaven's perspective, this was a successful night, even though it turned out differently than we thought it would. Julia responded to an invitation from Heaven and stepped out in faith, without knowing what the end result would be—and that is true success.

While I was a youth pastor, I would take my kids up to Bethel Church in Redding, California, to attend the Jesus Culture Youth Conferences. This was a special time because they knew that whenever we went to this event there would be a whole generation of young people gathered together to encounter the presence of God. When the presence of God would touch their lives, the youth were able to become an avenue of encounter for other people in the city.

As a youth pastor, I especially looked forward to this event because I was always able to take an extended time to connect with my youth in God's presence as well as have lots of fun. Most people that know me well understand that I am a "big kid" at heart. With that in mind, I always looked forward to the food fights, being drunk in the Holy Spirit, late night toilet papering, and the Holy Spirit chaos that went on surrounding the conference.

During one of the conferences, we all went to In-N-Out Burger after being blasted and filled with the power of God in a Jesus Culture "fire tunnel." (A "fire tunnel" is when the prayer ministry teams get into two single-file lines and face each other to form a "fire tunnel," through which the people walk as they receive prayer. The people praying lay hands on those walking through the tunnel and release an impartation of the fire of God on them.) At least half of my youth had to be carried from the van into the restaurant because they were too "drunk in the Holy Spirit" to walk.

Once we were inside, some of the youth were crawling on their hands and knees, praying for customers. I began to watch the customers get healed or touched by prophetic words. Some even joined in the laughter. As we left In-N-Out Burger, the junior high students begged us to take them to the emergency room to pray for people. These types of requests will always make a youth pastor's heart happy. Therefore, I had high expectations for the following Jesus Culture conference.

On the drive up, two of my 12-year-old junior high leaders wanted to talk to me. They explained to me, "We feel like its time for us to go to a whole new level in the Holy Spirit. In the past, we have seen many different types of pain and diseases healed. We have grown in the prophetic and words of knowledge, and we know that we are called to do everything that Jesus did. Jesus walked on water when He lived on the Earth, and we want to walk on water as well." (John 14:12 says, *"I tell you the truth, anyone who has faith in me will do what I have been doing. He will do even greater things than these because I am going to the Father."*)

As they told me this, I remembered all the times I had personally attempted to walk on water over the years. I began to chuckle as I reminisced about one night at the Crystal Cathedral in Orange County, California, where I thought I heard God tell me to walk on water. As people were walking out of church that evening, I shouted at the top of my lungs, "Everybody watch!" I was wearing dress clothes (also some really nice shoes) and was full of faith that when I stepped out into the pond that was right next to the footpath, I wasn't going to get wet.

For some reason I closed my eyes as I stepped out onto the pond. To my shock, I tripped over some rocks and fell face first into the water. Immediately, the security guards ran over to help me get up out of the water and began questioning me about what I was doing. I was so embarrassed, but explained to them that I was trying to walk on water.

As I recalled this story, their desire to do the same works as Jesus reawakened my faith to step out into the places where I hadn't yet seen breakthrough in my own life. I was extremely excited about their hunger and proud of them for telling me about it. I encouraged them that the perfect place to practice would be at my parents' pool (where they would be staying during the conference).

It turned out that every night, after the conference, we would have a big party at my parents' house. We would eat pizza, play games, and get drunk in the Holy Spirit. However, I kept noticing that the two guys who talked to me on the car ride were absent from the group time. I would look for them around the house and keep finding them outside by the pool praying to walk on water, (for a little over a half hour each time) and dressed in their regular clothes. They were not in their swimming shorts because they expected to walk on water and stay dry.

They really went for it, and for three straight nights they skipped the normal festivities and pressed into walking on water. However, each time they tried to walk on the water, they fell into the pool. After hearing the dryer running at night, I would joke with them the next morning at breakfast, "If you really had faith, you would keep your cell phones in your pocket when you stepped out to walk on the water." We all laughed and joked about it, but I knew that these guys were really catching the attention of Heaven.

After the conference, I decided to gather my youth group up and corporately celebrate these two revivalists for taking risk. I told everyone about what they had been doing, and as a group, we began to encourage and applaud their faith. Then, we all prayed for them to receive more faith and hunger from Heaven than they had ever experienced before.

One of my passions is to help facilitate a way of living that celebrates risk-taking. Naturally, it is easy to celebrate the testimonies of breakthrough when there is a physical manifestation of that evidence. However, I want to develop a culture that perceives risk-taking as the end result of success. Ultimately, those who take risks will catch the attention of the King. Heaven champions those who are willing to step out of the boat. Most of the time the risk-takers will not know the final outcome of their acts of faith before they step out.

Personally, I love hearing stories about breakthrough and healing. I hold a very high value for these testimonies because they can create momentum and build faith in others for God to do that same thing again. However, it is easy to create a culture of performance when the attention and praise is only given to those people who are producing results.

What about those who take risks that just don't pan out for them the way they thought they would? Our American culture teaches us that when we take risk and don't get the results we want, that means we have failed; yet I believe God sees risk-taking from a completely different perspective.

From Heaven's perspective, Papa God applauds us when we try new things and step out. In the very same way, a loving natural father gets proud and happy when his little baby takes her very first step and then falls down. Just like our heavenly Father, we as the Church must begin to acknowledge and encourage the ones who are taking those first steps, but have not yet seen their breakthrough happen.

Certainly, there will always be an uncomfortable tension for those who take risks without seeing results right away. But as we keep stepping forward into faith, we need to remember that we will see breakthrough when we partner with the Holy Spirit. Our ultimate goal is to remain in Him and become closer to the Vine (see John 15:1-4). It is imperative that we create a culture within the Church that doesn't just tolerate risk-takers, but encourages the whole Body of Christ to take risks in order to advance the Kingdom of God.

So, the day after we returned from the Jesus Culture conference, we did a beach baptism at Dana Point, California. A bunch of junior highers got baptized and afterward decided to pray together to walk on the water. They walked over to the water's edge, grabbed hands, and walked out into the water together.

As they took steps out into the water, they noticed that they were all about chest deep, standing on the ocean floor. However, one of the kids was still on top of the water! He took about five steps above the water and on the sixth step, fell into the water. Remarkably, he was one of the two guys who had been contending to walk on water in Redding several times that past week.

So then, if you try something for the first time and it doesn't work out, try again. This young revivalist knew what was available to him and kept trying until he saw breakthrough.

John Wimber prayed for hundreds of people before he saw someone healed. That is what this junior higher and John Wimber had in common: They were not basing their success upon their circumstances; instead, they were willing to take risk even when nothing tangible manifested. Bill Johnson often says, "We are not called to cultivate a theology based on our circumstances, but on the Word of God."

All of us have things that we are contending to see breakthrough for in our daily lives. We need to live in a level of faith that brings our circumstances in line with God's Word. When we take risk and don't see immediate results, we cannot lose hope and let thoughts of failure or inadequacy attack us because God sees risk-taking as success.

Another aspect of this principle applies to stewarding the gifts of the Spirit. Many people ask me specifically to pray and impart my healing gift to them. In response to their request, I sometimes tell them, "I can pray for you, but this impartation won't become activated in your life until you step out and begin praying for others." I don't necessarily believe that we can lose an impartation, but it can lie dormant if we don't activate it.

For example, everyone can have the gift of healing flowing from their lives and develop it by praying for the sick. The gift of healing, along with the other gifts of the Spirit that Paul speaks about in First Corinthians 12, is available to every believer.

Stewarding the gifts of the Spirit is like working out in the gym. When I was a freshman in high school, I discovered what it was like to work out in the gym. Up until that point, I had never experienced what it was like to lift weights.

I remember my very first day of working out. I was so determined to gain muscle mass that I worked out every muscle in my body for three and a half hours. When I lifted the bench press for the first time, I couldn't lift very much and felt like a wimp in front of all my high school classmates.

That night before going to bed, I put three scoops of my protein powder in my glass of milk and thought to myself, "It will only be a matter of days before I look like this guy on the protein powder container." I woke up in the middle of the night with excruciating calf muscle pain. I tried to stand up, but my body wouldn't let me. As I lay in bed, I tried not to move because when I did the pain got worse.

My body was going into rebellion and started telling me, "Chad, you should never work out again; you were not made for this." In the morning, however, I decided to push through the pain. I was inspired to get stronger and continue working out. Within a few months, I could bench-press more than double the weight than when I started, and I was no longer sore.

The same principle applies in the spirit realm. The more we exercise the gifts of the Spirit, the more breakthroughs we will ultimately see.

Many of us have attempted to operate in healing, prophecy, or other gifts, but have quickly become discouraged because we did not see results after the first attempt. Because we are made in God's image and likeness, we all have the capacity to reflect His manifold gifts and glory.

Michael Jordan, arguably the best basketball player of all time, was cut from his high school basketball team. His coach came to the conclusion that Michael Jordan didn't even have the talent level to ride the bench at the high school level.

After being cut, Michael had a decision to make: he could agree with his coach's assessment of his skills and go join the chess club, or he could improve his talent by doing his own drills and come back again the next year to compete. Instead of partnering with the coach's assessment, he went for his dream and developed his talent on his own. Clearly, Michael Jordan had talent from birth to play the game of basketball, but his talent did not come into fruition until it was joined together with a strong work ethic, discipline, and daily training. In a sense, he had to "work it out."

When people are full of faith and vision, they can see what is possible in the unseen realm. They will always contend for God-sized possibilities to become manifested in the present moment. When tenacious people come into an environment of lack, they can't help but tip the scales in God's favor and release breakthrough for a whole community. Tenacity is an attribute of faith.

When we pray, we release the Kingdom of Heaven, and that reality trumps every circumstance. Jesus told us in Matthew 4:17, *"Repent, for the kingdom of heaven is near."* Jesus' main message was about a Kingdom that was always within reach and tangible. We carry the same message of Jesus that cannot be reduced to just words, but must be reflected in our lives as we display the goodness of God through signs and wonders.

We need to believe in a God who acts on our behalf in the present, not in some far away and distant time, but now. He wants to come now and heal every time.

I remember a time in my life when I prayed for a man with cancer on a weekly basis over the span of several months. During this time, God asked me the question, "Are you praying at the same level of faith now as the first time you prayed for him?" When He asked me this, I hadn't changed the way I prayed externally. In fact, others were giving me encouragement about the faith I was displaying by continuing to diligently pray for his miracle to become manifest.

After God spoke this word to me, I took an evaluation of my heart and realized that I had, indeed, been praying from a lower level of faith than when I first began. God told me in response to my heart attitude that, "In order to live in a lifestyle of healing, you need to pray from the same place of faith, whether it is the first time or the thousandth time." I suddenly realized that I had a seed of unbelief that had crept into my heart, and it was up to me to weed it out.

Bethel Church has become a place where many people are healed of cancer after receiving prayer. On one particular weekend, a couple had flown in from out of town to receive healing prayer for the wife, who had been diagnosed with breast cancer. Over the course of the weekend, Joaquin and I spent several hours praying over and contending for her healing.

On Sunday morning, we prayed for her again after the service. We prayed every kind of prayer we knew, but were not seeing any breakthrough. Because it was getting late, we decided to take a break and go eat some lunch. We encouraged her that we would continue to pray for her when we saw her again at church that evening. As I left to get some lunch with friends, I felt somewhat defeated because I had put so much time and energy into praying for this lady and had seen no results.

As we started to receive our food, the same couple walked into the restaurant to eat lunch, along with my parents, and they sat down at the table directly next to us. My dad came over to ask me if I would take a minute out of my lunchtime to come and pray for the lady that I had been praying for all weekend. Everything inside of me, especially my stomach, wanted to say no because of the hot food in front of me. I wanted to explain to my dad that I had just prayed for her for several hours at Bethel over the weekend, and I wanted some time to just eat my food and take a break. I realized, however, that an opportunity had presented itself to me at an inopportune time.

In the midst of contending for breakthrough, there comes a point when it is inconvenient to pray again. In my experience, this is commonly the tipping point when God loves to move. God is looking for a generation that is always ready to respond to His voice and willing to be flexible in order for the Kingdom to be manifest.

I immediately thought to myself, *Wait, what am I thinking? I want to give God a platform to reveal His goodness.* I put aside my plate of food, and my whole table of friends went to pray for her. We all laid hands on her and released the Kingdom of Heaven. Suddenly, she sunk into her chair and started screaming because of the torment of fear she was experiencing.

Now, it is always our heart to release peace and not to expose the people we are praying for. My friend, Joaquin, knelt down and started releasing peace over her. She stopped screaming and started laughing uncontrollably.

The manager was watching everything unfold from the front door next to the hostess. He said to himself under his breath, "What in the world is going on here?" The hostess, who was currently enrolled in the school of ministry, heard what he said and told him that God was touching the woman, setting her free, and releasing joy over her. Her boss started confessing to her, "I am an alcoholic and very depressed." The hostess prayed for her boss and broke off the depression and alcoholism in Jesus' name.

After the laughing broke out at our table, the woman realized that she had no more pain and knew God had touched her. When we got back to our table, people came and asked if they could have the same joy that we were experiencing. We began to pray and tell people about Jesus.

Amazingly, after the couple flew back home, the wife went to her doctor and received test results back that she was cancer-free. Hearing the good news, I rejoiced and realized that God loves to come whenever and wherever we are. It does not matter how many times we pray for someone, but only that when we pray we believe that God will show up every time. That is the Risk Factor.

CHAPTER 8

Kevin Dedmon

THERE'S NO GOING BACK!

A few years ago, I had planned a one-day ski trip to Squaw Valley, California. Not wanting to ski alone, I asked a pastor friend, in the Lake Tahoe area, to assemble some local skiers to join me. In the course of our conversation, I mentioned that I liked to ski at the black diamond level and that I preferred to ski with people who were at an advanced level.

I was full of anticipation as I rode the gondola with the small group of skiers the pastor had arranged. My excitement quickly turned to anxiety, however, as I discovered that I had been set up with expert skiers who were into skiing ultimate extreme terrain.

One guy in the group regularly had film crews following him down the mountain because of his penchant for spectacular jumps off of 100-foot cliffs, as well as taking seemingly impossible routes through rocks and trees at death defying speeds. Another guy had been on the Squaw Valley mogul team and was an expert all-terrain skier. The other three seemed crazy enough to try anything that the first two might suggest!

I knew I was in trouble when I noticed that they all had helmets covering their entire face (like the ones used in a motorcycle moto-cross race). Conversely, I did not even have a partial helmet—just a thin knit beanie! The fact is, I had not planned on pushing the fear factor to the limit. I had anticipated something fun—safe. I did not need to prove my manhood on the slopes. I was hoping for the "yahoo factor," not the "oh no factor."

As we departed the gondola, one in the group suggested that we proceed to the "Head Wall" ski run. Attempting to appear calm to the group, I subtly inquired about the difficulty level. When I heard that it was rated as a double black diamond, my anxiety rose to mild panic because I had never skied at that level. Nervously, I began to reason that my contact had surely communicated that I wanted to ski on black diamond ski runs, not double black diamond!

As the chair lift brought us toward the top of the mountain, I began to feel slightly comforted, as I scouted out various run options that looked doable for my skill level. *Certainly*, I thought, *these guys are professionals—they are not going to put me in a situation above my ability.*

My panic, however, soon exploded into extreme terror as we exited the final chair lift at the top of the mountain and then skied underneath the crisscrossed bamboo poles reading, "Keep out, DANGER!" (You know, the signs that are intended to keep ignorant skiers from impending danger that communicate, "You're going to die!").

We quickly came to a stop, where I stood paralyzed by fear as my skies extended out over a ledge into thin air. My heart felt like it was going to explode through my parka as I looked down a 500-foot sheer steep, sprinkled with huge boulders, rock outcroppings, and trees that were gnarled up from constant exposure to high velocity winds and cold.

At that moment I thought, *I'm going to die.*

Then, I watched in horror as the others launched off of the ledge, jumping and flying over the obstacles below. All I could muster at that moment was a short, powerful prayer—"Help!"

God's answer shocked me; He said, "Yes, I'll help you; go for it!"

I could not believe my spiritual ears. "What do you mean, 'Go for it?'"

He said, "You have what it takes to get down this mountainside. Go for it!"

"But I have never skied something this extreme before," I replied.

Instantly, I mentally recounted many events throughout my life that had required various levels of risk to do what I had never tried before. Each time I had thought, *There is no way I can accomplish that—it's too crazy!*

This was the same fear I had felt the first time I stood up on skis and tried to ride the rope tow up the "bunny hill." It was the way I had felt when I advanced from the "bunny hill" to the "green" runs and then the "blue" and then the "black diamond." Each time I felt like I was going to die. Each time, fear almost kept me from going to the next level.

So standing on the ledge looking down at the others successfully negotiating down the mountainside hooting and hollering with joy,

I decided to ignore the overpowering panic, take a leap of faith, and just go for it!

There was an instant of terror as I launched off of the ledge, plummeting down the chute of snow-pack rimmed by boulders and gnarled trees. Incredibly, terror turned to an exhilarating adrenaline rush, however, as I negotiated the various obstacles seemingly stretching out to trip me up and cause me to crash to my death or serious injury. Surprisingly, I made it down in one piece. Thank You, Jesus!

Obviously, not all of us are going to take the kind of risk I took on that day (and probably should not), but all of us face fear factors at various levels and situations in life. For example, some of us face fear in trusting someone in a relationship. Others have to break through the fear barrier in going back to college when they are 40 years old.

Abraham certainly crossed the chicken line when he climbed the mountain to obediently offer his only son, Isaac, as a burnt offering to the Lord (see Gen. 22). I can almost hear him thinking to himself, *This is crazy! What am I doing? It took a miracle to get Isaac. If I sacrifice him, I'll never become the father of many nations!*

Fear was standing at the door of his destiny, trying to block him from the supernatural breakthrough that would propel him to be the father of nations as he was promised. Fear is always standing at the doorway of our destiny. The only way we will step into our supernatural destiny is by crossing the chicken line by breaking through the fear factor.

There is no doubt that Abraham would have never entered into his supernatural destiny if he had not taken the risk of obedience in offering his only son as a sacrifice to the Lord. Sure, he could have played it safe and kept the only son he had, but he trusted that God would provide. And sure enough, a ram was caught in the thicket and became the sacrifice for the burnt offering instead of his son. We are told that to this day it is said of that place of risk that, *"On the mountain of the Lord it will be provided"* (Gen. 22:14).

Too often we are waiting for the ram before we take the risk when the provision for the promise only comes when we obediently offer up sacrificial acts of risk. The good news is that God supernaturally provides in spectacular fashion when we break through the fear barrier and take risk.

In pursuing the prophetic promises God has offered, then, we must ask ourselves, "What mountain of risk is God asking us to sacrifice our fears on so that the promises God has made to us can be fulfilled?" In other words, "What are we willing to risk in order to open up the possibilities for God's supernatural intervention in our lives, and what actions will we take in order to step into our supernatural destiny?"

RISK REQUIRES A HUGE HEART

I loved the movie *Secretariat,* about a horse that won the Triple Crown of horse racing in 1973. There have only been 11 horses to win the three-race series since Sir Barton accomplished it in 1919. Amazingly, Secretariat set records in two of the three races (the Kentucky Derby and Belmont Stakes) that still stand today.

While the movie focuses on the journey of an amazing thoroughbred racehorse winning the Triple Crown, it is even more about a woman, Penny Chenery, who inherits her father's horse-breeding farm, but knows very little about the horseracing business. Her father's business had been profitable over many years, producing winning horses, but upon his death, Penny soon discovered that the farm was on the brink of financial ruin. With only one horse—Secretariat—left in the stable, the only option seems to be to sell the horse to a competitor breeder and racer in order to cover the backlog of bills.

Against all odds, and despite the efforts of her family to dissuade her, Penny literally risked the family farm and her family's inheritance, determining to race the horse herself instead of selling Secretariat to her competitor. She could have simply sold the horse to save the farm, but she believed that there was something special about Secretariat, prompting her to take unreasonable risk even though there was no apparent evidence to confirm her confidence.

Like many of us, she could have easily given in to the fear factor and stayed on the safe side of the chicken line, but she would have missed out on making history. It is only as we defy the odds, breaking the fear barrier, that we are able to accomplish the seemingly impossible and step into our supernatural destiny.

The veterinarian who did the autopsy on Secretariat estimated that the size of his heart was approximately 22 pounds, which is about two and a half times the size of a normal horse. Ironically, we would have never known the size of Secretariat's heart if Penny had not risked racing the horse to its full capacity. I do not know if they will ever do an autopsy on Penny when she dies, but my guess is that her heart is two-and-a-half times larger than the average human heart because of the size of the risk she took.

It takes a huge heart of passion to step into our supernatural destiny when others around us are trying to convince us to "play it safe." Furthermore, we will never know the size of our hearts until it is tested. Fear is the test that reveals the size of our hearts. When we break through the fear barrier, we find out just how big our hearts really are and how far we can truly go in our supernatural destiny!

In the parable of the man who hid his talent because he feared the master, Jesus points out that playing it safe is not tolerated in the Kingdom of God (see Matt. 25:14-30). The point of the parable is that those who refrain from risk will lose everything God had originally given them.

The fact is that fear tempts us to hold on to what we have, which eventually results in us losing out on our destiny. While fear prevents us from taking risk, the only way to get to our destiny is by taking risk. Therefore, in order to get to our supernatural destiny, we must be willing to walk through the fear barrier.

When I moved to Redding, California, to be part of Bethel Church in 2002, I took a huge risk. My wife, Theresa, and I had been pastoring a church that we had planted in Huntington Beach, California, for the previous ten years. We owned a house close to the beach and loved all of the amenities of beach culture. Moreover, we had led hundreds of people to Christ through the many community outreaches we had developed and led over the years, and we enjoyed a tremendous amount of favor in the city as a result.

There was something burning in our hearts, however, for an expression of the Kingdom of God that was demonstrated in supernatural power, as opposed to merely relying on the great strategies and programs that we had labored under for all of those years. We knew there was more for us, and we also knew we were going to have to do something radical in order to get to the next level of our destiny.

Through the years, we had received many remarkable prophetic words promising that we were called to be world-changers having international influence. Prominent prophetic people had called me out by name, along with private personal information, conveying my part in one of the greatest revival harvests in history.

Hearing these prophecies, I had thought that they would be self-fulfilling—if they were from God, they would automatically come to pass. Years later, however, I realized that I had to partner with the prophecies I had received. I finally understood that they were invitations into the "more" that I had desired, and in the end, I had to take some kind of risk to access the power to propel me into His promises for my destiny.

Interestingly, the greater prophetic potential we have in our destiny, it seems like the greater level of risk we must take in order to step into our destiny. In other words, small risk results in a small measure of our destiny being fulfilled, while extreme, even dangerous levels of risk result in world-changing impact. Now, what seems like little risk for one person is dangerous risk for another. Risk is risk, as I explained in my earlier chapter on "The Supernatural Nature of Risk."

In my journey, I found that I had to take a significant level of risk in order to partner with the prophetic words given me. We decided that resigning our church, selling our house, and moving to Redding, California, was the risk level we needed to take in order to be launched into our supernatural destiny. To our friends and colleagues, our risk looked like an absurd adventure into stupidity. I really cannot blame them. We did not have a job lined up at the church, or for that matter, any job.

Our plan was to use the equity accrued in our house in Huntington Beach to take a year's sabbatical while we attended the Bethel School of Supernatural Ministry. Once again, this plan seemed ludicrous to my pastor friends, who reminded me that I already had a Bachelor's degree in Biblical Studies and a Master's degree in Church Leadership Studies and that the Bethel school was not even accredited!

Basically, it appeared as though I was giving up everything I had worked for to pursue a nebulous, uncertain future. Nonetheless, I knew that Bill Johnson and Kris Vallotton had charted some essential Kingdom breakthroughs and core values that I needed in order to get to the next levels of my destiny.

Certainly, I felt a tremendous amount of fear in deciding to move, but like Penny and Secretariat, we must grow a huge heart in order to enter into the huge plans and purposes God has prepared for us. Today, I am living my dream because I broke through the fear barrier and crossed the chicken line in taking a level of risk that seemed unreasonable to others.

FEAR IS FOUNDED IN OUR FOCUS

Our focus determines our direction, and our direction ultimately determines our destiny. When we focus on fear, it becomes an obsession that deters us from our God-given destiny. In Hebrews 10:38, we are told that, *"My righteous one will live by faith. And if he shrinks back, I will not be pleased with him."* Going backwards in risk-taking is never a legitimate option for the believer in fulfilling his or her supernatural destiny.

In the context of the Book of Hebrews, the Jewish Christians were being tempted to give up on their faith in Christ because of the persecution the Church was experiencing at that time. They were afraid because they focused on impending doom for their future, instead of the promises of God's goodness. Throughout the letter, the writer exhorts these Hebrew Christians to continue in the direction they originally determined by keeping their eyes on Jesus (see Heb. 12:2).

Fear causes us to shrink back from the supernatural destiny God has for us. Whether fear is based upon a real threat or a false perception of reality, we must break through the fear barrier in order to fulfill all that God has for us.

I'll never forget the time I took my son, Chad, who was 14, and his friend, Mark, to hike up Rattlesnake Canyon in the Jumbo Rocks Park near 29 Palms, California. The hike was a three-mile unmarked scramble though giant boulders over a gain of about 3,000 feet in elevation.

We were into the hike about an hour when we came to a precarious section in which the only route we could find was to straddle and shimmy up an A-framed-shaped boulder positioned up at a 45-degree angle, stretching across a 75-foot-wide canyon that dropped down about 150 feet. Halfway up the sharp-edged granite boulder, with legs dangling over each side, my son's friend started to freak out as he began to focus on the long fall if he was to slide off the edge.

He began yelling, "I'm going to die! I can't make it!" His eyes were wide with fear as he began to look for a way to shimmy back down the way we had come. He began to yell at my son, who was behind him, to turn back. Instantly, my son began to partner with his friend's fear.

Immediately, I knew we were in trouble as their emotions escalated into unbridled panic, and Mark began to yell at Chad to go back down the incline. Now, it is usually a bad idea to back down a steep incline in such a precarious circumstance. It was difficult enough shimmying forward—the risk of falling was greatly enhanced going backward. One slip would lead to certain death.

Just as Mark was about to try and turn around to go back the way we had come, I swiveled my torso, grabbed on to his shirt at the chest, and demanded that he look into my eyes. I could see the terror, as tears were welling up in his widened brown eyes. Firmly, I told him that going back was not an option. His eyes said *no* as he shook his head in disbelieving shock, breathing like he had been doing wind sprints.

I continued in earnest, "Fear is not an option right now. I need you to focus on me and slow your breathing down." I immediately matched his breathing and then coaxed him into slower and slower breaths until his breathing rate normalized. Continuing to look him in the eyes, I explained that we were going to proceed forward and that I wanted him to keep his eyes on me and nowhere else.

Amazingly, we shimmied up the remaining distance without incident and nervously laughed together in relief that we had made it without anyone dying.

Interestingly, it was not the incline and sheerness of the boulder that presented the danger, resulting in an irrational response of fear (climbing it was like riding a granite horse). Rather, focusing on the distance to the ground below us conjured up feelings of impending doom.

Whenever we focus on things incongruent with our prophetic destination, our perspective shifts and we encounter abnormal fear that dominates and derails us from our destiny. Mark was doing fine climbing up the boulder until he took his eyes off the final destination and looked down. His shift in perspective paved a pathway into fear that could only be rerouted as he refocused on the objective.

Similarly, when Peter stepped out of the boat and began to walk on the water, he was doing fine until he saw the wind. He became afraid and began to sink only after he changed his perspective, taking his eyes off the Lord and focusing on the threat. Wisely, he cried out, *"'Lord, save me!' Immediately Jesus reached out His hand and caught him."* Then He admonished him saying, *"You of little faith...why did you doubt?"* (Matt. 14:22-31).

Lack of vision creates doubt, and doubt leads to fear, and when fear dominates us, it derails us from our supernatural destiny. Thus, it is only when we are walking toward Jesus with our eyes on Him that we are able to walk on the water of the supernatural in extreme faith. In negotiating the precarious pathways through life, we must keep our eyes fixed on the author and perfecter of our faith (see Heb. 12:2).

FOCUSING ON FEAR DERAILS DESTINY

Hawaii is one of my favorite spots in the world. Having spent a lot of time riding the waves of Huntington Beach, California (officially known as Surf City), I especially enjoy the perfect waves and warm tropical water of Hawaii.

Several years ago, my wife and I had the opportunity to spend 12 days on the island of Kawai. I was really looking forward to body boarding some of the great breaks on this dreamy small island.

There was a certain surf break that required a few hours of driving, but that promised the best waves. Sure enough, arriving, we found a nice-sized, two-foot overhead reef break that barreled perfectly, providing a spectacular "green room" encounter with each ride.

Three local surfers who had been enjoying the ideal conditions for several hours before I had arrived accompanied me on this isolated surf break. After about 30 minutes, they casually announced that it was dinnertime, and that they had to leave. Thinking it was rather strange that they would be going to dinner at 2 P.M., I asked why they would be going to dinner so early. One answered, "Oh, we're not going to dinner—it's time for the sharks to start feeding." At that, they left without any further explanation.

Now, I had read that there were white tip sharks in the area, but I could not remember reading anything about a certain feeding time. So, now I was out in the ocean by myself, and the locals had left because it was "dinnertime," and I was left wondering whether they had just pulled a local prank on the tourist as they had finished their surf session or they were giving me a friendly "heads up."

Waiting for the next set of waves, all I could hear in my mind was the music theme from the movie, *Jaws*. I took a few more waves, but after ten minutes, I could not deal with the overpowering anxiety as I thought of becoming the entrée of an impending shark attack. The waves were epic, but I was a nervous wreck. Overwhelming fear completely dominated my every thought, no matter what I tried to do to counteract it.

I finally succumbed to the fear and rode the next wave into the beach. I spent the next hour watching the perfectly breaking waves from the safety of the beach without seeing a single shark in the water beyond. To this day, I really believe that there were no sharks near that surf break.

That is the thing about fear. It does not even matter if the point of fear is real or not—if we believe the threat is real, then we will respond accordingly.

The enemy uses fear to keep us from our destiny. When David was walking through the valley of the shadow of death, he said, "...I will fear no evil..." (Ps. 23:4). From his perspective, death was just a shadow—not true reality. The enemy is always trying to trick us into believing that a threat is true, trying to prevent us from taking the level of risk that will propel us into our prophetic promises.

Even when the threat is potentially dangerous, we are not to be ruled by fear when it interferes with our destiny. The Lord is very clear on this point, *"Do not be afraid for I am with you..."* (Isa. 43:5).

Israel almost did not go into the Promised Land because of fear of the real threat of the giants. Thank God for Joshua and Caleb, however, who saw the truth that God with them was more powerful than the giants of fear. Maybe they heard the words that God later asked the Israelites through the prophet Isaiah: *"...Who are you that you fear mortal men, the sons of men, who are but grass?"* (Isa. 51:12).

Jesus demonstrated the proper way to deal with fear when He and the disciples were caught in a life-threatening storm on the Sea of Galilee in which the disciples believed they were going to die. *"He said to them, 'You of little faith, why are you so afraid?' Then he got up and rebuked the winds and the waves, and it was completely calm"* (Matt. 8:26).

Jesus faced the same kind of threats that we face, but He dealt with them from a perspective of faith, evidenced by risk that released the miraculous intervention of Heaven into the circumstance. The storm only has the power we give it.

I want to encourage you to begin to speak to the storms you are facing. It will not be long until you break through the fear barrier

REFOCUSING RELEASES RISK

Our focus determines our destiny. When we focus on the enemy, we have already lost the battle, because we have allowed fear to dominate us. I believe that is why the apostle Paul taught that *"we live by faith, not by sight"* (2 Cor. 5:7).

Perfect love drives out fear (see 1 John 4:18). Jesus is the epitome of perfect love. When we keep our eyes on Him, fear is not an issue, and we can do all things through Him who strengthens us (see Phil. 4:13). Many people try to fight the devil of fear by speaking directly to it. I have found, however, that the best way to defeat that enemy is by not looking at it—ignoring it. When I act as though it does not exist, I find that I am free to focus on and pursue my prophetic potential.

When I play golf, there are numerous obstacles on the course intended to breed fear. I find that when I focus on the hazards, I tend to hit into them. I used to pull out a "water ball" from my bag every time I came to a hole that had water in play. Amazingly, I could hit those balls into the water from any position on the golf course. If water ran parallel with the fairway, I would shank it into the middle of the pond. If I was required to hit over it, sure enough, I would skull my ball into the middle with three or four skips.

Finally, I decided that I needed to take drastic action in order to overcome these formidable obstacles. I committed to using my precious Titleist Pro V golf ball. Then, pretending that there was no hazard, I only focused on my target. Amazingly, I began to successfully negotiate the hazards. As a result, I lowered my scores substantially and saved a lot of money on golf balls in the process!

When Jonathan attacked the Philistine outpost at Geba in First Samuel chapter 13, it ignited a response in which the Philistines assembled 3,000 chariots, 6,000 charioteers, and soldiers as numerous as the sand on the seashore. Conversely, the Israelites, under Saul's command, only had a total of 3,000 soldiers—they were overwhelmingly outnumbered.

We are told of Israel's response in the following passage,

> *When the men of Israel saw that their situation was critical and that their army was hard pressed, they hid in caves and thickets, among the rocks, and in pits and cisterns. Some Hebrews even crossed the Jordan to the land of Gad and Gilead* (1 Sam. 13:6).

Notice that when they *saw* the enemy, fear set in. When we focus on the enemy, we lose sight of God's ability to provide supernatural intervention in the face of insurmountable odds, and then, it is not long until we are hiding in fear, debilitated from our destiny. Later in this passage, we are told that only 600 soldiers were left to protect Israel's future (see 1 Sam. 13:15).

In the next chapter, however, Jonathan fearlessly attacks the Philistines again, saying to his armor-bearer, *"…The Lord has given them into the hand of Israel"* (1 Sam. 14:12). We are told that Jonathan only killed about 20 men, but as a result, God instigated a panic that struck the entire Philistine army so that they began to run in every direction (see 1 Sam. 14:14-15).

After this, *"When all the Israelites who had hidden in the hill country of Ephraim heard that the Philistines were on the run, they joined the battle in hot pursuit"* (1 Sam. 14:22). When they refocused their attention on what God was doing, they lost all fear, enabling them to take radical risk, and the Lord rescued Israel that day (see 1 Sam. 14:23).

It only takes one person to refocus, break through the fear barrier, and take one act of risk in order to impact the rest of the culture and to change its focus and come into their destiny. That person could be you!

The apostle Paul preached fearlessly in the name of Jesus even though his life was at risk (see Acts 9:27). In his letter to the Ephesians, however, he sought empowerment to overcome fear when he asked,

Pray also for me, that whenever I open my mouth, words may be given me so that I will fearlessly make known the mystery of the gospel, for which I am an ambassador in chains. Pray that I may declare it fearlessly, as I should (Ephesians 6:19-20).

When we break through the fear barrier, it paves a way for others to follow and take risk for themselves. The apostle Paul pointed out that, because of his breakthrough, *"...most of the brothers in the Lord have been encouraged to speak the word of God more courageously and fearlessly"* (Phil. 1:14).

In Psalm 34:4, David testifies *"I sought the Lord, and He answered me; He delivered me from all my fears."* I want to encourage you that God will answer when you call on Him, and He will help you break through your fear barrier so that you can step across the chicken line and enter into your supernatural destiny.

SECTION 5

STEPPING INTO YOUR SUPERNATURAL DESTINY

CHAPTER 9

Chad Dedmon ⟫ **OUR CEILING—
YOUR FLOOR**

L iving in the realm of faith releases us to step into our destinies. In order to accomplish this, it is vital that we surround ourselves with relationships that encourage and challenge us. I love to surround myself with people who are more on fire than I am. I remember growing up as a leader in my church and encouraging those around me to go after God. Although I enjoyed encouraging people around me, I would often feel alone in my level of hunger as I pursued God. There were many times when I felt drained as I would pour into others' lives and help them out. In my heart, I longed to be a part of a community where everyone was seeking God with the same intensity and passion.

When I first arrived at Bethel, I felt a fresh wind of the Holy Spirit, and I heard God tell me, "This is a place of grace where you are free to be who you are." From that point on, I felt the embrace of God where He wooed me into a place of intimacy with Him. Also, I finally felt the power of living in a community of believers who had like hearts. I was part of a tribe of people with one voice, sound, and mission on the Earth. As I began to realize that this was a safe place for me, I was released into a lifestyle of risk like never before.

The Body of Christ is designed to be the first place where we learn how to experiment and take risk in the supernatural. If we find ourselves restricted when taking risk in the church, where friends and family surround us, then we will never step out of the four walls of the church to represent Him.

Once I was at Bethel, God gave me a group of friends who I took risk with, and we also learned how to dream big God-dreams together. It was commonplace for us to connect on a deep level and share our prophetic destinies with each other.

I remember one night we were at a local restaurant telling stories of what God had done throughout the day. At the end of the meal, my friend Bobby asked me if I wanted to go to the hospital and pray for the sick with him. I said that I was pretty tired and that I felt like going home to watch a movie. He looked over and reminded me of a prophetic word I had received a few months earlier about clearing out hospitals. He invited me to step into my destiny right then and start healing people in hospitals that very night.

If I had been eating alone or with friends who were not concerned with calling out the destiny in one other, I would have gone home and finished the night with a bowl of ice cream. Instead, I had an amazing friend who was inviting and pushing me to step into my calling. So, we went to the hospital and saw several people healed. Then, we finished off the night with a bowl of ice cream.

Possessing big dreams in our hearts is important for our growth, whether our dreams involve preaching in open-air crusades to thousands of people or bringing our whole family to the Lord. We need to be able walk in our dreams in the present day and not live with the mindset that we will only accomplish our dreams in the distant future. It says in Zechariah 4:10, *"Who dares despise the day of small things?"*

Maybe we have received a prophetic word that we are going to "preach in open-air crusades to the multitudes." I would like to suggest that if we have the mindset that God is going to fulfill this word on His own without us taking steps toward this dream in our everyday lives, we are mistaken. We need to take the steps to prepare ourselves for the fulfillment of the prophetic words we have received in practical ways. If we expect some big ministry to call us on the phone to say, "We would like to invite you to Africa to preach in a stadium to 100,000 people," that phone call probably will never come.

I would encourage you to live with the mindset of beginning to look for opportunities in order to steward and take risk to step into your dreams every day of your life. So, if your dreams are to do open-air crusades, then go find where there are people who need a touch of Jesus today in your community. When you share with your co-workers the love of God or heal someone in the grocery store, as you are walking away, just tell yourself, "This is just the beginning of my open-air crusade ministry. I am living in my dreams."

To illustrate this point further, I want to share a song from one of my favorite singers, Dave Mathews. He wrote a very prophetic song called "You Might Die Trying." Here are the lyrics:

To change the world,

Start with one step.

However small,

The first step is hardest of all.

Once you get your gate,

You will walk in tall.

You said you never did,

Cause you might die trying,

Cause you might die trying.

Cause you—

If you close your eyes,

Cause the house is on fire.

And think you couldn't move,

Until the fire dies.

The things you never did,

Oh, cause you might die trying,

Cause you might die trying.

You'd be as good as dead,

Cause you might die trying,

Cause you might die trying.

If you give, you, you begin to live.

If you give, you begin to live.

You begin, you get the world.

If you give, you begin to give

You get the world, you get the world.

If you give, you begin to live.[1]

This song describes how we begin to generate the momentum to change the world by taking risk. Dave Mathews articulates that for people called to live in their dreams, the beginning steps are the most difficult, but also the most important. In the chorus, Dave makes the point that we might not ever end up taking risk because of the possibility of failure.

It is imperative that we focus on the rewards of risk and not the downfalls. The bridge of the song is probably one of best bits of music to play for an offering time at a church service, "If you give, you, you begin to live. You begin, you get the world." That lyric about living our lives as offerings and serving others blew me away. It is the reason that we take risk, not for our benefit, but for the benefit of others, so that they can live in the breakthrough of Heaven.

There is another person in my life who consistently calls me into my destiny, and that person is my wife. We go on a date night once a week, and it is common for us to prophesy or heal the sick on our date nights. On one date night, while I was pastoring, I had several meetings during the week, and was looking forward to having a relaxing time with my wife by sharing a nice meal out. My wife usually has impeccable timing, and she will have to use the ladies' room right before our food comes out.

On this particular occasion, the waiter set down before me the two plates of hot food while she was gone in the restroom. I decided to be a gentleman and wait for my wife to get back before I started eating. Looking over in the direction of where she would be walking back, I saw her talking to some people at another table and praying for them. My initial response was, *What is she doing? This is date night, not ministry time.* Then the thought came to me that this was the life that we had signed up for—releasing the kindness of God wherever we go and, in doing this, making the choice not to compartmentalize our lives. I decided to push aside the food and get up to join my wife in praying for the people at the neighboring table.

This lifestyle in our marriage began on our first date. I took Julia out to a nice Italian restaurant followed by a romantic walk where I turned to her and said, "I want to love Jesus with all of my heart and release the Kingdom of Heaven on Earth for the rest of my life." I asked her, "How does that sound to you?" She gave me a beautiful smile and replied, "Sounds good to me; that's what I want to do, too."

We decided to end our date by going to one of the most romantic places in Redding, the emergency room of the hospital. When we arrived, we immediately noticed a man, who had second-degree burns on the upper half of his body, waiting to see the doctor. After a few moments of prayer, he started feeling a cool wind on his skin and an itching sensation. All the pain he had been experiencing was gone as the nurse called his name to come in and see the doctor.

We looked around for more people to pray for and saw a woman who had a broken ankle that was ballooned up with swelling and discoloration. As we began to pray for her, the ankle began to lose its discoloration and shrink down to normal size. She got out of her wheelchair and started running around the emergency room shouting, "Thank You, Jesus." We prophesied over her friend, and she got saved. What a wonderful first date night.

Inviting spiritual fathers and mothers to pour into your life is necessary for you to be catapulted into your destiny. One quote that I love on this subject is Bill Johnson's, "My ceiling is your floor," which directly refers to the sons and daughters of God receiving their spiritual inheritance from their fathers and mothers. In other words, the next generation can take off and build from the past generation's level of breakthrough. I have found it vital to have many fathers and mothers in my life.

Paul told us in First Corinthians 4:15, *"Even if you had ten thousand guardians in Christ, you do not have many fathers...."* Some people interpret this Scripture as one of the crutches of the Church, thinking it means that we will always be in position of not having many fathers. I believe Paul was telling the Body of Christ that there needs to be a shift in the Church where the number of fathers overtakes the number of teachers.

My natural parents are never threatened as I pursue and invite spiritual fathers and mothers into my life; in fact, they respond in quite the opposite way. They understand the value in cultivating many of these important relationships. I greatly desire to invite fathers and mothers into my life who aren't only for my spiritual life, but transcend into every facet, including in my marriage, finances, risk-taking, surfing, and so forth.

One of the cornerstone principles that I learned at Bethel is *to place value and honor on what fathers and mothers have stewarded throughout their lives.* You can find this principle taught on in Matthew 10:41, *"Whoever welcomes a prophet, as a prophet, receives a prophet's reward...."*

One of the Greek origins for the word *honor* is *value.* So then, if you connect your heart to what the prophets are carrying and have contended for throughout their lives, you can receive their "gift" and "reward" freely.

Before I met Julia, I took a couple out to lunch who were in ministry and had lived out a loving and nurturing marriage for over three decades. As a single man, I wanted to prepare myself to be able to understand how to cultivate a great marriage in the midst of ministry. I asked them several in-depth questions about what they had done to live out a balanced lifestyle of marriage and ministry.

Toward the end of the lunch, they asked me, "Chad, are you getting ready to ask somebody to marry you?" I chuckled and said, "No, I'm just a hopeful romantic, setting myself up for success for when I do find the woman of my dreams."

The Bible says there is wisdom in a multitude of counselors. I try to invest myself in relationship with people who have wisdom in different areas before I ever need to draw upon their counsel. If and when a time comes when I need their advice for a certain situation, I have already invested in the relationship long before I need to rely on them.

When you are a pastor at a church, you are being constantly pulled into others' life emergencies. Unfortunately, most relationships like this begin out of someone's need and not out of two people beginning a natural friendship. Many times in the Church, people are trying to draw on accounts where they have never invested anything. Picture relationships like an ATM transaction; you need to have equity in your account before you try to make a withdrawal so you don't go into debt.

In this whole place of inheritance, I would like to share a story of one of my spiritual mothers, Heidi Baker. She has mentored me in the faith realm and the miraculous. Several years ago, she received a prophetic word from Randy Clark about coming into a season when she would have authority over blindness.

After receiving that prophetic word, she took whatever measures necessary to pray for blind people; she even once stopped in the middle of traffic to pray for a blind person. I was able to observe her tenacity during that season, and I was in a place of awe each time that occurred, as I watched her tap into the faith realm with total confidence, believing that it was the moment the prophetic word would come to pass.

After two years of this occurring and seeing no physical break-through of blindness being healed, she called up the blind in a meeting, yet again. A woman responded who was blind, and Heidi prayed with the same faith as she had the two previous years. After a moment of prayer, the woman was completely healed of blindness. Heidi was surprised to find out her name was Mama Aida, the very same name Heidi is known by in Africa. Additionally, the next two women that Heidi prayed for who were healed of blindness were all named Mama Aida.

Several years later, my wife and I were in Fiji doing ministry. One late night, thanks to the invention of Skype, Julia and I spoke to Heidi while she was ministering in California. We had a great time of praying, connecting, and laughing together. The next morning, I was preaching, releasing the Kingdom of Heaven and calling out words of knowledge for healing. Many people responded, but one in particular was a blind woman. I laid hands on her for a moment, and she said she felt fire and heat in her eyes, so I said, "You should check out your eyes to see if there is any improvement." To her surprise, she opened them to find her vision completely restored. I asked the lady her name, and she said, "Mama Aida."

There are no coincidences in the Spirit realm. It is not happen-stance that I had been talking to Heidi the night before. She had cultivated an authority over blindness, and then, after speaking with her, I saw a blind lady healed hours later who had the name, Mama Aida. We were in Fiji for a month and did not meet another person with the name Heidi or Mama Aida. As a spiritual son, I was able to receive freely Heidi's authority over blindness, for which she had contended to have authority over for years.

I have also discovered that when I am with my friends, we see greater outbreaks of the Spirit than when I am alone. There is a Kingdom principle that when there is unity in the Spirit, it releases a greater anointing for breakthrough. David writes in Psalm 133:1-2, *"How good and pleasant it is when God's people live together in unity! It is like precious oil poured on the head...."* Individually, I can take risk and release outbreaks of the Spirit, but it is way more fun to partner together with friends. God is releasing a new wineskin for how ministry is accomplished—in a team and friendship setting.

For example, when hurricane Katrina occurred in 2005, a group of my friends got together and all went to the Houston Astrodome in order to minister to the victims of the disaster. Years earlier, we would often sit around and dream about the day when we would be in stadiums together praying for the multitudes. When the opportunity came, we knew we had to "strike while the iron was hot." So, even though we all had full-time jobs, we decided to drop what we were doing and make arrangements to meet up in Houston.

We had no idea how we would gain access into the stadium; we just booked our flights and trusted that God would open up the doors. As we were walking through the parking lot, we were told by some people that we had to be certified Red Cross workers or be a part of a media team in order to enter into the facility. We further learned that the stadium was on lock-down, and they kept people from coming and going for health and safety reasons.

We did not meet any of those qualifications—we just had a heart to come in and serve, pray for people, and partner with the Holy Spirit to see breakthrough come to these precious people. In a high security situation like this, one would logically think that we would not want to draw attention to ourselves, but that was definitely not the case with our group of friends. As we approached the entrance, one of our team members started shouting out, "Revival! God's on the move! Glory!" Another team member was walking around and openly displaying his camcorder (which was off limits).

Both of these occurrences got me thinking, *We are going to get denied access for sure after all this noise and commotion.*

We walked up to the front gate to go through the line and sure enough, the National Guard security officer told us, "You cannot come in here because you don't have the right qualifications, and you have a camcorder video recording device, which is not allowed." Feeling somewhat deflated and discouraged, we all started walking back to our car; then I suddenly remembered a prophetic word I had received before I left for the trip.

Some friends of mine had told me that when we arrived at the Astrodome, the door would be closed, but the next door to the left would be open. Initially, I interpreted this word to mean a spiritual door, but in that moment I realized that it was a literal door. I told the team, "Let's try to get in through the next door on the left." So, we walked up to the security guards at the next gate, and they ushered us right through with no questions asked.

This was truly a miracle! Our excitement grew exponentially as we prayed to see what God wanted to do. Right away, we met a lady who was bedridden in her cot who had three herniated discs. She let us lay hands on her back and pray. She told us that she was feeling electricity in her back. We asked her to check it out, and to our amazement, she got up right out of her cot and started touching her toes and had full range of motion in her back. She was so overjoyed that she began to scream, "Look at this, I couldn't do this before." She became our evangelist and was shouting out to everyone around in the general vicinity, "Look at this, I am healed! You need to have these people pray for you."

She walked over to a man in a wheel chair and brought him over to us, all the while convincing him that if we were to pray for him, he would be healed. While we were praying for him, my friend Chris Overstreet saw a lady with a wrist brace walking by and proclaimed to her, "Excuse me ma'am, God is healing your wrist right now." She immediately took off her wrist brace to check it out and realized that there was no pain.

People began gathering to receive prayer and as I looked up, a huge smile spread across my face as realized that I was back-to-back with my friends ministering to the crowd of people just like we had dreamed about years earlier. There were many people passing by and watching this crazy scene take place.

There was one lady in particular who was walking by, and as she entered the scene, she was instantly slain in the Spirit without anyone touching her. A police officer rushed to her side to find out what happened to her. Calmly, Chris Overstreet walked over to the officer and exclaimed, "It's OK officer. God is touching her." What we didn't realize was that there was a portal of God's Presence that continually intensified and touched people all around this area. Unknowingly, the lady had walked right through the center of this portal and got touched by the Holy Spirit.

After a few minutes, the lady came to, looked at us, and started confessing that she was an alcoholic. She explained that she had not drunk anything in the past few days, so she was experiencing alcohol withdrawals and sickness as a result. She told us, "Whatever it was that just touched me is the answer for my life." We started praying for the spirit of addiction to leave and for her to be filled with the Spirit. She began laughing uncontrollably and started rolling around on the floor exclaiming, "It feels so good."

While this was happening, we discovered that the first lady, who was first healed in her back, was a grandmother, and her daughter and granddaughter had been sitting and watching everything that had been taking place. I started talking to the daughter and had an open vision of her as a 5-year-old girl. I explained to her that the Father wanted to heal something that happened to her when she was 5-years-old. With tears streaming down her face, she began to receive the Father's love. I asked her, "Do you want to know Jesus as your personal Lord and Savior?" She responded, "Yes, as long as you pray for my daughter as well to know Jesus (who was also 5-years-old).

Just as they started praying to receive Jesus, the grandmother walked over and said, "I want to know this Jesus, too. Don't leave me out!" So the whole family prayed together to receive Jesus. In that moment, I took a step back and was in awe of everything that God did in just a few minutes. I got to literally watch people be healed, delivered, and saved, all in a matter of minutes.

After this happened, we decided to pair off and pray for the various people inside the Astrodome who needed healing. Chris Overstreet and I were paired up, and we immediately found a lady who had been in a car accident and was living in a wheelchair. Two years earlier, her spine had been severed, and she was no longer able to walk. Chris and I began to pray for her, and the power of God started flowing into her spine.

Right then, a man walking by screamed out at me, "What did you just do to me? You did some kind of voodoo thing to me." A little taken back by his demeanor, I thought to myself that something supernatural must have happened to him for him to respond in this way. I replied, "What happened to you?" He explained that as he was walking by, he felt a surge of energy and electricity go through his knees and, furthermore, that he had had two failed operations on his knees. So, I told him, "Move your knees around and check them out." He began jumping in the air and doing leg squats, testing out his knees, and he started laughing, telling me, "I feel like I have new knees; there is no more pain or restriction!"

I explained to him that what he had just experienced wasn't voodoo; rather, that it was Jesus who healed him because He loves him. We turned our attention back to the lady in the wheelchair, and we asked her to check it out. She got up out of her wheelchair on her own initiative and walked hundreds of feet for the first time in two years.

After spending several days in the Astrodome, we saw many outbreaks of the Spirit occur. These were only two stories of many that happened during this time. My friends and I found ourselves saying, "Isn't it amazing that we are alive right now to witness what God is doing?" We started pinching ourselves, realizing that our dreams were becoming a reality right before our eyes. It is amazing what can happen when friends get together to release revival.

Lord, right now I release favor and grace to discover the spiritual fathers and mothers that You have called people to connect with, those who live in their backyard. I pray for Jonathan and David friendships to begin to form as they knit together their hearts and dream together with trusted friends whom You have given for their encouragement. In Jesus' name, amen.

ENDNOTE

1. David Matthews, "You Might Die Trying," *Stand Up*; http://www.azlyrics.com/lyrics/davematthewsband/ youmightdietrying.html; accessed September 9, 2011.

CHAPTER 10

Kevin Dedmon ⟩⟩ OVERCOMING COW'S

During my senior year of high school, I was required to meet with the school counselor to discuss my college and career options. After studying my transcript, she advised me not to even consider college, but to apply for a job with the city in the sanitation department. Her reasoning was that I would always have a job because there would always be garbage to pick up, and the pay and benefits from the city would provide me a decent living.

I barely graduated from high school. I was not stupid—I just was not a good student. I did not like school. I liked to play, so I never really studied. I was smart, however, in that I would make friends with people who were smart and would bribe them to let me copy their homework and give me answers for tests.

I had a dream a few years ago that the school board determined that my diploma was invalid because I had not actually done the work. They ordered me back to high school.

In the dream, I was 40 years old, dressed in a business suit, and carrying a brand new leather briefcase. Frantically, I looked for my first class, too embarrassed to ask one of the kids where the room was hidden. Everyone gave me a knowing look that I had cheated the first time through and had been busted. What a nightmare!

When I became a Christian, I read my first book—the Bible. It took about a year to finish it, even though I read at least an hour a day. I immediately discovered a love for the Scriptures and found the truths readily applicable to my life. I would imagine myself as the various Bible characters I read about, trying to live my life the way they modeled. Soon, I knew that I wanted to live my life in total surrender and service to Christ and His work.

I had been a Christian for about a year when I met Theresa. We had drawn each other's names as prayer partners at her parents' Catholic Charismatic prayer meeting, and a year and a half later, we were married. We both felt a divine calling to full-time career ministry, so after a lot of prayer and research, we decided to save enough money to attend L.I.F.E. Bible College in Southern California, where Jack Hayford was president.

I'll never forget, being 20 years old, married nine months, and driving our Volkswagen station wagon loaded up with everything we owned, from Reno, Nevada, to the middle of Los Angeles. I remember being so excited about preparing for my career in full-time pastoral ministry. Even better, Theresa and I had all the same classes, which helped me feel more comfortable in such a spiritual and academic environment.

Two weeks into Bible college, we were told that that we had a week to prepare for our first exam. I studied more in that week than I had studied cumulatively throughout my entire high school experience—about six hours. I confidently took the exam, thinking I would surely get my first A.

When our tests were returned to us at the beginning of the next class, I was shocked to see that I had received a C-. Theresa received a 100 percent! I could not believe it—we had studied the same amount. To make matters worse, the professor called Theresa and three others, who had also scored 100 percent, to the front of the class.

The professor told the class that the four who had scored 100 percent were to be looked at as role models for the class; they were the leaders who would be the examples to the rest of us. Then he looked at me, shook his finger, and said, "And you, Kevin, you should be more like your sister." I thought, *My sister! You're 80 years old, and about to see Jesus face-to-face after I lay hands on you!* I had never felt so humiliated and embarrassed in my life as the professor went on to say that my "sister" was a great role model for me to follow after.

When the class dismissed, I told Theresa that I was quitting school and headed toward the admissions office to try to get my money back and go back to Reno and work with my father as a carpenter. Theresa stopped me, encouraging me not to make a rash decision. She began to console me, pointing out that I had never studied in my life and that I just needed some time to acclimate myself to an academic environment. After several hours of her prodding, I determined to break through the fear barrier of failure, take another step of risk, and give school one more try.

I studied about ten hours for the next test, and was shocked when I got the test results back—100 percent! I eventually transferred to Vanguard University in order to pursue an even more challenging academic environment, and amazingly, graduated with a B.A. and an M.A. degree, with a 3.94 grade-point average.

Today, I am sort of a garbage collector. I find people who think they are garbage and bring them to the greatest recycler in the universe—God. He then recycles and transforms them into world-changers.

DESIGNATED FOR A DESTINY

Each one of us has a supernatural destiny. We are called to be world-changers and historymakers, revivalists who are called to bring the Kingdom of God to Earth through the manifestation of God's goodness and kindness, demonstrated in signs and wonders, miracles, healings, and prophetic insights that call out the gold in people and reveal the good plans and purposes that He has for each person.

As believers, we have the same supernatural destiny as the first disciples Jesus chose. In Luke chapter 6, we find the process and purpose for which Jesus chose the 12 disciples:

Jesus went out to a mountainside to pray, and spent the night praying to God. When morning came, He called His disciples to Him and chose twelve of them, whom He also designated apostles (Luke 6:12-13).

Notice that they were *called* disciples (learners, students), but *designated* apostles (sent ones, world-changers). In other words, they had a destiny that went beyond simply learning about Jesus and following Him. They were called to go out and change the world, making disciples of all nations (see Matt. 28:19).

Jesus is inviting us, like the disciples, to step into our supernatural destiny—to partner with Him in bringing Heaven to Earth. The only thing required on our part is to take risk, crossing the chicken line to release the presence and power of Christ that resides within us (see Col. 1:27).

I am sure that the disciples felt very unqualified with the designation Jesus gave them as apostles—sent ones. They were unschooled, ordinary men (see Acts 4:13) who probably felt intimidated by the thought that one day they would be doing the miracles that Jesus modeled.

In the same way, when we hear that we are world-changers and historymakers, it is easy to feel overwhelmed with the promise of such a seemingly grandiose destiny. After all, it often seems like only "special" people have that call on their lives.

While it is true that Jesus intentionally chose 12 disciples from among the multitude that followed Him, we are all chosen to represent Him to the world around us (see 2 Cor. 5:20). He chose the 12 after a night spent on a mountain, and He chose us after a night of prayer in a garden—the Garden of Gethsemane (see Matt. 26:36-46).

Just as Jesus saw the *PP* (prophetic potential) in each one of the 12 that He called disciples and designated as apostles, so too, He sees our *PP* and invites us into partnership with Him—to step into our supernatural destiny.

At some point, then, we must step across the chicken line to find out our true supernatural potential. In Luke chapter 9, we find the account of Jesus sending out the 12 disciples to demonstrate their destiny.

We are told that,

> When Jesus had called the Twelve together, He gave
> them power and authority to drive out all demons and
> to cure diseases, and He sent them out to preach the
> kingdom of God and to heal the sick...So they set out
> and went from village to village, preaching the gospel
> and healing people everywhere...When the apostles
> returned, they reported to Jesus what they had done...
> (Luke 9:1-10).

Amazingly, they came back with testimonies of their success. *I'm
sure they were thinking, We are world-changers. We really do have what
it takes to be historymakers. We are healing revivalists. We do have a
supernatural destiny!* The only way to find out how much we have
been equipped and empowered is to be activated in a risk adventure.
Like the disciples, we will never know how much of Christ is in us
until we release Christ through us in risk.

DERAILED BY DISAPPOINTMENT

A few days later, however, the disciples were confronted with a
COW (a constraint, challenge, obstacle, offense, or weakness) that
threatened to derail them from their destiny. Later in Luke chapter
9, we read,

> A man in the crowd called out, "Teacher, I beg You to
> look at my son, for he is my only child. A spirit seizes
> him and he suddenly screams; it throws him into
> convulsions so that he foams at the mouth. It scarcely

ever leaves him and is destroying him. I begged Your disciples to drive it out, but they could not."

"O unbelieving and perverse generation," Jesus replied, "how long shall I stay with you and put up with you? Bring your son here." Even while the boy was coming, the demon threw him to the ground in a convulsion. But Jesus rebuked the evil spirit, healed the boy and gave him back to his father. And they were all amazed at the greatness of God... (Luke 9:38-43).

The disciples could not drive the demon out. Wait a minute! He had just given them power and authority to drive out *all* demons, yet they could not help this boy? They could not, or would not? Maybe they tried once or twice and then gave up. Whatever the case, they stopped taking risk at some point, and when they stopped taking risk, they were derailed from their destiny.

In Luke 10, we find these words, *"After this the Lord appointed seventy-two others..."* (Luke 10:1). Why did Jesus appoint others? I believe it was because the original 12 would not go out again! They had experienced a disappointment and become discouraged, resulting in disillusionment that derailed them from their supernatural destiny.

How many have prayed for people for healing, only to have them not respond or even die? How many have tried to lead someone to Christ, only to be personally rejected? How many have made efforts to change an environment to be more Kingdom-like, only to be ostracized as a fanatic?

So many have had dreams of doing great things for God, only to have them dashed by disappointment. When that happens, our dreams turn into daydreams, and we are derailed from our destiny.

DISAPPOINTMENT TO DESTINY

I once prayed for a woman with cancer, and she died. I thought I killed her because I was not gifted enough, did not have enough faith, and was too arrogant to ask someone else pray for her— someone who was more gifted and full of faith. As a result of the heart-breaking disappointment, I became discouraged, disillusioned, and derailed from my destiny as a healing revivalist.

For 23 years after that disappointing experience, I did not pray for the sick. I believed in healing—I even taught about healing as a pastor, but if someone wanted to be healed, I would direct him or her to someone who I believed was gifted. When they insisted I prayed for them, I responded that my prayers would be at the least, ineffective, but that most likely the person would get worse or even die!

In 2000, we had a roommate, Joe, who had a serious back injury, which left him bed-ridden for about three months, and constantly writhing in pain. One night, we had a leadership meeting at our house, and Joe asked to be carried out into the living room, thinking that being around people would help him take his mind off of the pain.

After the meeting, he pleaded with me to pray for his healing as he lay on the couch in excruciating pain. I explained that I should not pray for him and that no one else on the leadership team was gifted for healing either, but he continued to press the request. Finally, I relented out of sheer pastoral compassion, and I asked two of our leaders to help him stand up.

I put my right hand on his lower back where the injury was located, hoping that he would not get worse. Immediately, I felt a fire on the palm of my hand, as Joe yelled out, "My back is on fire!"

He began to jump around the living room, repeatedly yelling, "I can't believe it! I'm healed, I'm healed!" I was more shocked than he was, but finally, I assured him that he was healed, especially after he started doing karate kicks and jumping around with wild abandon.

The other leaders began asking for me to lay my right hand on them to be healed of various ailments. Each one was healed as I placed my still burning hand where they needed healing.

I have been releasing healing on people ever since. As a result, I have seen thousands of people healed since that night in 2000.

I heard Jack Hayford once say, "You never fail when you fall. You only fail when you don't get back up." We must commit ourselves to working through our COWs to get to our PP.

From my perspective, many world leaders have seemed to be people who are the least likely to succeed. Many have had to work through some kind of handicap hindering them from being world-changers. One of the common threads in their development toward their destiny, however, was that they have taken risk to overcome their COWs to achieve their PP.

I love the story of King George VI of England, who was portrayed in the movie, *The King's Speech*. Utilizing a speech therapist, he overcomes a stammering problem, which prepared him to effectively communicate to the people of England when the decision was made to declare war on Germany, starting World War II. His risk in working through his COWs rallied the people of England to rise up into their destiny to help Israel.

I want to encourage you that whatever your COW is in pursuing your PP, the Holy Spirit will help you overcome and will inspire you to step into your supernatural destiny.

DRINKING OURSELVES INTO OUR DESTINY

In Acts 2, we are told that,

> When the day of Pentecost came, they were all together in one place. Suddenly, a sound like the blowing of a violent wind came from heaven and filled the whole house where they were sitting. They saw what seemed to be tongues of fire that separated and came to rest on each of them. All of them were filled with the Holy Spirit and began to speak in other tongues as the Spirit enabled them (Acts 2:1-4).

Further in the chapter, the disciples were demonstrating the effects of the Day of Pentecost out in the community, and the response was that, *"Some...made fun of them and said, 'They have had too much wine'"* (Acts 2:13). In response to this accusation,

> Peter stood up with the Eleven, raised his voice and addressed the crowd: "Fellow Jews and all of you who live in Jerusalem, let me explain this to you; listen carefully to what I say. These men are not drunk, as you suppose. It's only nine in the morning! No, this is what was spoken by the prophet Joel: 'In the last days, God says, I will pour out my Spirit on all people...'" (Acts 2:14-17).

I want to suggest that the disciples truly became apostles when they got drunk on the Day of Pentecost, enabling them to step across the chicken line into their supernatural destiny.

My son, Chad, and I were speaking at a Supernatural Lifestyle conference in England a few years ago. We were training about 250 people in healing, the prophetic, and supernatural evangelism. In that context, we had set up a time for everyone to go out on a Treasure Hunt to activate the conference attendees in what they had been learning about their destiny as world-changers.

The Treasure Hunt is an evangelistic strategy that I developed utilizing a "treasure map" constructed through words of knowledge (clues), and consisting of five categories: a location, a person's name, a person's appearance, the areas of their life that they need miraculous intervention, and anything unusual, not fitting into the other four categories. We then use these clues to find the hidden "treasures" (people) within the community and give them a taste of the goodness of God through healing and prophetic ministry.

The pastor hosting the conference informed me that we would probably only have about 20 people willing to go out on the Treasure Hunt. He reasoned that the English are more concerned with proper social etiquette, precluding them from approaching strangers in public. I explained to him that we crazy Californians are just as reticent in approaching people. The fear of man crosses most cultural boundaries.

I assured him, however, that most of the people would go out on the Treasure Hunt once I had properly trained them. When he asked how I would pull off such a miracle, I said, "I'm going to get them drunk!"

Sure enough, people got so filled with the Spirit (see Acts 2:13-17; Eph. 5:18) that they forgot about the fear barrier, and stepped into their supernatural destiny. About 225 of the attendees went out on the Treasure Hunt, and many of them came back with amazing testimonies of how God had used them to heal, prophesy, and lead people to Christ throughout the community.

Chad and I took out the leadership team of the church hosting the conference. One of the names I had on my Treasure Map was "John." As we walked along a row of sidewalk restaurants, I began asking men if their name was John. After six "no's," I became discouraged and determined not to ask anyone else. In fact, I decided that I was not going to look for any more clues. Period. I had experienced enough rejection in the strange looks that communicated, "You're a weirdo," to derail me from my destiny.

Sulking and feeling sorry for myself over experiencing so many rejections, I followed the rest of the group down the street about ten yards behind. I passed by a group of five young adults drinking beer at a sidewalk café. A few steps past, the Lord spoke to me and said, "Go back and ask whether one of their names is John." I immediately said no. Once again the Lord said, "Go ask." I said, "You go ask! I would have to be really drunk to subject myself to another rejection."

Instantly, I became drunk with His presence. Without thinking, I turned back toward the young people at the sidewalk café. When I arrived, I asked, "Excuse me, but is anyone here named John?" One of the three guys sitting closest to where I was standing on the sidewalk, said, "Yeah, my name is John."

Immediately, his two guy friends at the table began laughing, saying, "Your name isn't John." Now, I am thinking, "Thanks a lot, God. You sent me back here to play a joke on me! This Treasure Hunt is getting worse by the minute!"

"John" looked up at me and said, "Well, my middle name is John. What would you do to me if my first name was John?" Recognizing this as a Divine appointment, I confidently answered, "If you had something wrong with your body, I would heal you. Do you have anything wrong with your body?" He answered no, and then thought about it more and said, "Yes, I have itchy ankles." I thought,

Is this guy for real? But then I asked, "How long have you had itchy ankles?" He said, "About six months." Aghast, the two other guys at the table looked at "John" and asked, "Is this something that is communicable?"

Just then, Chad came up to the group and asked if any of them had a lower back problem because he had that ailment as one of the clues on his Treasure Map. One of the guys said that he had pain in his lower back. Chad then asked if he had a leg shorter than the other, and after checking, he found that he did.

As Chad grew the leg out, causing the guy's back to be healed, I was praying for "John's" itchy ankles. After about 30 seconds, all of the redness left, and "John" exclaimed, "All the itchiness is gone!" He was completely healed.

Immediately, a few of the other leaders with us began calling out clues of ailments that they had on their Treasure Maps. Both of the girls at the table were instantly healed of headaches, and one girl's neck was healed as the leaders prayed for them.

I figured it was time to go to the next level, and I asked the group if they wanted to meet Jesus, who had just healed them. They thought I was referring to a Hispanic guy. They had never been to church nor read anything in the Bible, and they knew nothing of Jesus.

I asked "John" to put his hands out and say, "Come, Holy Spirit." He held out his hands and repeated the words as I placed my hands on his. A few seconds later, he began laughing hysterically, shouting, "What are you doing to me?" As he continued to laugh, I went to the guy whose back had been healed and asked if he wanted to feel God's presence. He said yes and held out his hands without any prompting. With my hands on his, he invited the Holy Spirit, and began to laugh. Now he and "John" were laughing together. I went to the third guy, and he held out his hands, and just like the others, began to laugh as he repeated, "Come, Holy Spirit." One of the girls also responded with ecstatic laughter when she spoke the words.

When I asked the second girl in the group if she wanted some, she contorted her face, and said, "No way, this is weird." "John" immediately broke in, "Go ahead and let him give it to you. It will be the best thing you have ever experienced!"

Reluctantly, she held out her hands and said, "Come, Holy Spirit," while flipping her head back in a way that communicated that this was a waste of time. Soon, she began showing signs of a smile. "John" broke in, saying, "Oh, here comes the laughter." Immediately, the girl broke into laughter, igniting a new wave of laughter among the group. Our group joined in, and all of us encountered a breakout of the joy of the Lord at the sidewalk café.

It is often very easy to quit right before the breakthrough. I have found that the best way to truly step into my supernatural destiny is to continue taking risk regardless of the results. I have found that the best way to continue in taking risk is by being continually drunk in the Spirit (see Eph. 5:18).

There is no way to get breakthrough without pressing through the COWs into the PP that God has purposed for us. I have found God faithful in doing His part when I continue to do mine.

In closing, I would like to encourage you with the words of the apostle Paul when he said,

With this in mind, we constantly pray for you, that our God may count you worthy of His calling, and that by His power He may fulfill every good purpose of yours and every act prompted by your faith (2 Thessalonians 1:11).

The only thing that is keeping us from our supernatural destiny is the Risk Factor! Go for it! Cross the chicken line!

About the **AUTHORS**

Kevin Dedmon has a traveling ministry focused on equipping, empowering, and activating the Church for supernatural evangelism through signs and wonders, healing, and the prophetic. He earned a Master's degree in church leadership and has been in full-time ministry for more than 25 years. He and his wife are part of Bethel Church staff in Redding, California.

Chad Dedmon has full-time pastoral experience working with youth and young adults. Chad and his wife, Julia, were ordained as ministers of the Gospel of Jesus Christ by Drs. Rolland and Heidi Baker of Iris Ministries and Senior Leaders Bill and Beni Johnson of Bethel Church. They reside in Orange County, California, and travel worldwide as ministers.

IN THE RIGHT HANDS, THIS BOOK WILL CHANGE LIVES!

Most of the people who need this message will not be looking for this book. To change their lives, you need to put a copy of this book in their hands.

> *But others (seeds) fell into good ground, and brought forth fruit, some a hundred-fold, some sixty-fold, some thirty-fold* (Matthew 13:8).

Our ministry is constantly seeking methods to find the good ground, the people who need this anointed message to change their lives. Will you help us reach these people?

> *Remember this—a farmer who plants only a few seeds will get a small crop. But the one who plants generously will get a generous crop* (2 Corinthians 9:6).

EXTEND THIS MINISTRY BY SOWING
3 BOOKS, 5 BOOKS, 10 BOOKS, **OR MORE TODAY,**
AND BECOME A LIFE CHANGER!

Thank you,

Don Nori Sr., Founder
Destiny Image
Since 1982